I0540386

Anti[conventional] Thinking

Also by Jeffrey Baumgartner

The Way of the Innovation Master

The Insane Journey

Anticonventional Thinking

The Creative Alternative to Brainstorming

Jeffrey Baumgartner

J P B
www.jpb.com
Erps-Kwerps, Belgium

To the memory of my father, Gerald Baumgartner

CONTENTS

INTRODUCTION

Anticonventional thinking (ACT) is a way of thinking in which you purposefully reject the conventional in favour of the unconventional in order to be more creative.

A few years ago, I do not remember exactly when, I became increasingly frustrated about brainstorming. For decades, it has been the business standard for generating ideas, which is fine except that brainstorming is not an effective way to come up with truly creative ideas as I will explain in the next chapter. Research has shown this, my experience has shown this and frustrated managers who have experience with brainstorms know this.

Moreover, if you watch a team of truly creative people – such as artists, composers or scientists – collaborate on a creative project, you will see that what they do is not at all like brainstorming.

Nevertheless, brainstorming has remained the norm for business idea generation since probably before you were born! Creativity consultants by the truckload swear by it and swear at me for daring to suggest that their beloved thinking method is anything less than perfect. Ironically, they seem to feel that brainstorming should be embraced and used simply because it is the way they have been doing things for years; an attitude that should be an anathema to a creativity proponent.

I feel otherwise. In 2010, I started working on an alternative. I looked into the research into why brainstorming does not work. I read studies on how the brain stores memories, recalls memories and constructs ideas. I read up on how groups of people collaborate. Then I looked at how artists, writers and other professionally creative people collaborate on projects. Here, I have an advantage. I am an artist by training and an author by trade. Over the years, I have collaborated with exceptionally creative people, and in doing so, have experienced marvellous peaks of creativity. However, the artist's approach to creative collaboration breaks just about all the rules of brainstorming.

The result is anticonventional thinking, which is in part a philosophy on how the mind works and, in part, a process that people in business, government and other organisations can learn to apply in their innovation processes.

Anticonventional thinking goes against a lot of the accepted standards in business creativity. But, please bear in mind two things. Firstly, many of those accepted standards are derived from creative problem solving (CPS) which is an expanded and more elaborate process based on brainstorming and unproven assumptions about creativity. Secondly, businesses for the most part have, thus far, not demonstrated a propensity for creativity. So, maybe it is time to change those standards!

That's kind of what this book and ACT are about.

Before I can explain ACT, let us look at why brainstorming does not work.

THE PROBLEM WITH BRAINSTORMING

BRAINSTORMING IS FUN
BUT NOT CREATIVE

Brainstorming is great fun, good for team building and a self-esteem builder. However, it does fail in one rather important way. It is not very good at providing you with creative ideas. It is even worse if you want a highly creative idea that you will actually implement.

The first thing we need to do here is to clarify what I mean by brainstorming. The word has two meanings. The first is as a generic term for generating ideas. This is how it is most widely used. But within creativity circles, brainstorming is a specific process devised by Alex Osborn, an advertising chap, in the 1940s. He later wrote about brainstorming in several books on creativity. He also teamed up with Sidney Parnes to develop a more sophisticated creativity approach known as creative problem solving (CPS), which has been institutionalised and is still revered at the International Center for Studies in Creativity at Buffalo State College.

Our interest is with Mr Osborn's method. Let's take a look at how it is supposed to work.

BRAINSTORMING IN A NUTSHELL

Brainstorming as defined by Alex Osborn and as practised by many a creativity facilitator in the decades since is a simple process:

1. A facilitator writes a problem statement on a whiteboard, chalkboard, flipchart or similar.

2. A group of brainstormers is invited to shout out ideas. All ideas are welcome, and no ideas may be criticised or questioned. To do so is the ultimate sin. Thinking freely is encouraged.

3. At the end of the idea shouting phase, ideas may be clustered to combine similar suggestions and a best idea or set of ideas, is chosen. Mr Osborn was vague about how to choose. Often the brainstormers are asked to vote for the best ideas.

CPS has built upon this, most importantly by emphasising the importance of analysing a problem and formulating an effective problem statement before getting to the idea shouting bit.

Surprisingly, when you consider that creativity is all about trying out new ideas and embracing change, brainstorming has remained largely unchanged since Mr Osborn invented it based on a series of assumptions that he made while running his ad agency! This is even more surprising when you consider that these assumptions have largely been proven wrong over the years.

THREE INTRINSIC FLAWS OF BRAINSTORMING

Brainstorming has three serious flaws that prevent it from being very effective as an idea generation method:

1. A group of people shouting out ideas is less creative than the same people writing ideas individually.

2. Reserving judgement and prohibiting criticism reduces creativity.

3. Decision makers (and others) tend to choose moderately creative ideas over highly creative ideas.

Critics and defenders of brainstorming tend to focus on the first flaw; which is a pity. It is the least damning and most readily mended problem with brainstorming.

The second two flaws are far more serious and cannot easily be solved without radically changing the concept of brainstorming.

FLAW 1: THE GROUP THING DOES NOT QUITE WORK

In 1958, a team of researchers at Yale University was one of the first to test brainstorming[1]. They put together several groups to generate ideas. Half of the groups followed Osborn's method and collaborated to generate ideas. The other half were nominal groups in which each member simply wrote down ideas without interacting with others in the group. All groups proposed ideas for the same problem.

When reviewing the results, the researchers found that the nominal groups consistently had more ideas and more creative ideas than the brainstorming groups.

Subsequent tests have confirmed the Yale researchers' findings. Fortunately, however, for the brainstorm facilitator, it is not a difficult problem to get around. For instance, you can have people write down ideas individually for a period before putting the individuals into groups to combine the individual ideas and then generate more together. So, this is a valid criticism of the original method, but not a serious impediment. The other criticisms are far more serious.

FLAW 2: CRITICISM ENHANCES CREATIVITY

The fundamental rule of brainstorming, of course, is that there is to be no criticism or questioning of ideas. Instead, all ideas are to be welcome irrespective of how boring or irrelevant they may be. Criticising ideas will hurt people's feelings and inhibit their creativity. This assumption sounds really good. So good, in fact, that it was not even tested until recently. But when it was tested, it was also found to be flawed.

A couple of researchers at the University of California, Berkeley[2] set

---

1   DW Taylor, PC Berry and CH Block, "Does Group Participation When Using Brainstorming Facilitate or Inhibit Creative Thinking?" Administrative Science Quarterly 3, no 1 (1958): 23-47
2   Matthew Feinberg, Charlan Nemeth (2008) "The 'Rules' of Brainstorming: An Impediment to Creativity?", Institute for Research on Labor and Employment Working Paper Series (University of California, Berkeley) Paper iirwps-167-08
    http://escholarship.org/uc/item/69j9g0cg

up three sets of brainstorming teams. One set was given no instructions. The second set was given traditional brainstorming instructions and specifically told not to criticise ideas during idea generation. The third set was given brainstorming instructions with difference. This set was specifically encouraged to criticise ideas during the idea generation phase. Most of the teams in the traditional brainstorming set moderately outperformed the teams in the set given no instructions. But the teams specifically told to criticise ideas consistently came up with the best results by far!

This bit of research appals most brainstorm facilitators and lovers of CPS because it breaks the fundamental rule of both methods: criticism is not allowed during ideation. Any hint of criticism, they claim, will cause participants to clam up, become inhibited and stop sharing ideas. But, as the Berkeley research has shown, this is not the case. Criticism actually enhances the level of creativity. Moreover, when I have encouraged criticism in ACT, participants have really liked it. As one man said, "When we are allowed to criticise ideas, we can really question them and understand them better." This is true. You cannot truly build upon an idea without questioning it, and you cannot question it without criticising it.

Frankly, I am not surprised by the results. When I think about my artistic collaborations, the idea generation process was never like traditional brainstorming. It was an argumentative debate. Ideas were criticised, questioned in detail and thrown away if they were not good enough. Seemingly silly ideas, once defended became core ideas to the project. Ideas that were boring were promptly rejected.

Criticism Adds Value to an Idea

Less obviously, criticising an idea gives that idea value. Think about it. If you suggest an idea and it is simply documented on a list, you have no idea whether anyone really cares about the idea. However, if a participant of your idea generation session stops and questions your idea, she is granting it importance. She is, in effect saying, "Your idea is interesting enough that I want to talk with you about it and understand it better."

FLAW 3: PEOPLE DO NOT LIKE CREATIVE IDEAS

Because the aim of brainstorming is to produce a large number of ideas, the result of any brainstorm will be a long list of ideas that someone needs to sort through in order to identify which idea or ideas to take forward. Brainstorming does not address this task. CPS is vague. In practice, there may be a vote for best ideas. In any event, ideas are often organised in some fashion and presented to a manager who must make a decision. You would assume that the manager would be eager to choose the most creative ideas.

But the truth is, in spite of what they say, people do not like creative ideas very much. Research at the University of Pennsylvania[3] has demonstrated that people are actually biased against creative ideas. Given a choice of ideas to implement, most people will select relatively conventional ideas over more creative ideas. This is doubly true if evaluation criteria are vague (such as "choose the best idea"). What this means is that, even if against all odds a brainstorm results in a truly creative idea buried among the many mediocre suggestions, that creative idea will be ignored in favour of one of the less original suggestions.

Of course, the manager is not consciously prejudiced against the most creative ideas on the list. Rather, when she sees them, she may feel they are too weird, she may believe they would be overly demanding to implement or, because of their originality, she may simply not recognise their value.

---

3   Mueller, Jennifer S.; Melwani, Shimul; and Goncalo, Jack A., "The Bias Against Creativity: Why People Desire But Reject Creative Ideas" (2011). Articles & Chapters. Paper 450.

My Experience

My own experience reinforces the research: brainstorming is ineffective as a creative process. That experience includes facilitating brainstorms in my dark and distant past as well as talking to innovation managers, around the world, who have been frustrated by the often useless results brainstorms bring. For them, brainstorming not only fails to deliver results, but it is a time-consuming waste of resources.

Brainstorms, I find, tend to capture a large number of mediocre ideas that are praised because that is what one does in a brainstorm. The result is that people feel good about submitting low-quality ideas. This is doubtless one reason why they remain popular: participants feel good afterwards.

I have also found that brainstorms tend to capture a lot of "buzzword" ideas. A buzzword, in a corporate context, is a particular word or phrase that often uses jargon that becomes fashionable in an organisation. Buzzwords typically have little meaning but are used widely. For example, at the time of writing, popular buzzwords include: "big data," "internet of things" and "selfie." Large organisations typically co-opt popular buzzwords internally as well as coin their own buzzwords.

Whether or not buzzwords are a good thing, you can be sure that they will find their way into corporate brainstorms. For instance, "incorporate big-data into the solution," might sound good in any brainstorm, but it is so vague as not to have any real meaning.

Worse still, buzzword ideas are often voted as the best ideas in a brainstorm, perhaps because they are fashionable.

In short, I find that brainstorms generate mediocre ideas and buzzwords, both of which are complimented, thus rewarding brainstormers for thinking conventionally and, therefore, discouraging unconventional, divergent and creative thinking.

I have also noticed that many a manager tends either to file away the brainstorm report without acting upon it, or she goes ahead with ideas that existed prior to the brainstorm, using the brainstorm report, which inevitably includes those ideas, to legitimise her decision.

GOOD FACILITATOR

Champions of brainstorming often like to argue that brainstorming is, in fact, very difficult to do well and requires a well-trained facilitator who fully understands all the complexities of brainstorming and CPS.

When they say this, I believe they are short selling themselves. It is not that brainstorming is a great method, but only in the hands of the right facilitator. Rather, a good facilitator can still make a flawed method work reasonably well.

A talented chef working with tinned food can still make a good meal of it. But she can make an even better meal out of fresh ingredients. Likewise, a talented creativity facilitator can get good results from a brainstorm. But she could get much better results out of a better method.

IN SHORT

In short, brainstorming is an ineffective way to develop creative ideas. This is widely recognised, especially among innovation managers and others who have actually tried brainstorming for their own needs. However, until now, no one has developed an alternative to brainstorming that truly addresses the three main flaws of brainstorming and the current research into creativity and the brain. Until now.

ANTICONVENTIONAL THINKING IN A NUTSHELL

WHAT IS ANTICONVENTIONAL THINKING?

Anticonventional thinking (ACT) is a way of programming your mind to reject conventional thinking in favour of unconventional thinking when you need to be creative. ACT is unconventional both in terms of how people think and in terms of veering from traditional creative thinking techniques such as brainstorming and CPS.

ACT is a thinking process in which you identify a situation where you want to take creative action, analyse that situation in depth, build associations between the situation and other things (such as situations, people, emotions, just about anything) and then build a creative vision of an action you might take in that situation.

ACT differs from other creative thinking processes in the depth to which you explore a situation and that the aim is to build a big, unconventional, creative vision rather than a long list of ideas.

ACT was originally designed as a collaborative activity with these four steps:

1. Play with the situation.

2. Develop a sexy goal (Optional).

3. Build a creative vision.

4. Implementation plan.

You will find a detailed explanation of these steps in **The Method** section of this book.

ACT can also be used by an individual working alone, in which case the sexy goal is probably not necessary. The individual can simply flow from playing with a situation to building a creative vision.

In order to understand why ACT works, we need to look at how the mind remembers things and imagines things – two surprisingly similar and related processes.

HOW YOUR MIND REMEMBERS AND IMAGINES

THE CREATIVE POWER OF YOUR MIND

In order to understand why ACT is the best creative thinking approach since the dawn of the human race, it helps to understand how the mind forms ideas. To do this, we first need to understand how the mind forms and recalls memories.

So, let's remember something and see how it works. To do this, I would like you to think about a talk you have recently had with a friend. Stop and remember it for a moment, then answer these questions:

Who did you talk with?

What did you talk about?

Where were you?

What was happening in the background?

How did you feel about the conversation at the time?

How did your friend feel?

What did it smell like?

WHAT HAPPENED?

Your memory is not like a camera that records your life as a long film which you can rewind and fast forward in order to recall experiences. Rather, as you go through life, experiencing stuff, learning, reading, assuming and forming ideas, your mind collects and processes all of these experiences; breaks them down into small chunks of memory – let's call them notions, and stores the notions in an orderly fashion across your entire mind. Thus, notions about your friend are kept in one area of your mind. Notions about emotions are in another area of the mind. Notions about smells are in another area. And so on.

In short, your mind is a kind of crazy, multidimensional database in which notions are stored in a structured fashion for easy retrieval.

THOUGHT CONSTRUCTOR

When you remember something, a mechanism in your mind – let's call it the "Thought Constructor" – quickly fetches the relevant notions and strings them together in order to recreate a memory for mental playback.

When I asked you to recall the talk you had with your friend, the Thought Constructor found the relevant notions and pieced them together to form a vision in your mind. Initially, the Thought Constructor probably put together only the basic pieces you needed to recall the event: basic notions about your friend and details of the conversation.

As I asked you questions about the conversation, the Thought Constructor had to find additional notions to make the memory more complete. For instance, unless the smell at the time was an integral part of the conversation, you probably did not recall the smell until I asked about it. But when I did ask, it was no problem for your mind to add the smell to the memory. However, you were probably not recalling the actual smell at the time of the conversation, but a notion of the smell you would normally associate with the environment where the conversation took place.

No one understands exactly how or why the Thought Constructor works. We simply know that it does work, and it is what enables us to recall memories, be they life experiences, knowledge or even feelings.

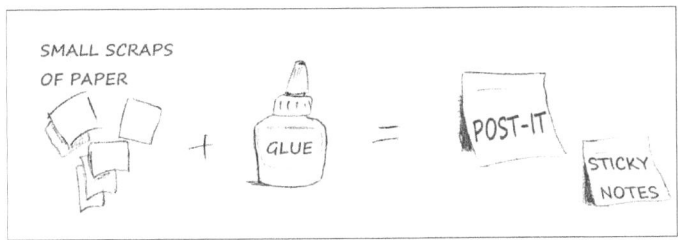

BUILDING CREATIVE IDEAS

Visualise the conversation again, but this time imagine that while you and your friend are talking, a cat walks past, looks up at you and asks, "Excuse me, but have you seen a mouse run past?"

Now, I am assuming that there were no talking cats involved in the experience. Moreover, I assume you have never encountered a talking cat in real life, though you likely have come across them in cartoons.

Nevertheless, your mind has sufficient information, tucked away in the form of notions, to change the memory of the conversation and include a talking cat. Indeed, if you close your eyes and let your imagination run for a couple of minutes, you could probably visualise you and your friend responding to the cat and then to each other about the cat.

REALM OF IMAGINATION

We have moved from the realm of memory to the realm of imagination where creativity resides. Nevertheless, the process of visualising things in your imagination is pretty much the same as the process for visualising memories: your Thought Constructor whizzes through your mind, retrieves various notions and tries to connect them in ways that make sense.

If the connection of two or more notions results in an all new notion, at least as far as your mind is concerned, you have built a creative idea. If your mind likes the idea, it becomes an established notion that can be used for constructing new creative ideas in the future.

This is what creativity is all about: connecting existing notions to create new notions.

Of course, the typical mind tends to focus notion retrieval on information related to the situation for which it is looking for a creative idea. For example, you are camping in a secluded area on a rocky hill. You have brought canned food to eat, but realise you have forgotten to bring a can opener. You are hungry. So, you try to come up with an idea. Your Thought Constructor will most likely retrieve notions about cans, how can openers work, the strength of a can and the things in your environment you might use to open the can. The Thought Constructor would be unlikely to retrieve notions about sofas or capital cities in Europe. These notions are irrelevant to the situation.

As a result, you might have the idea to find two stones, one with a strong, pointed edge and a large one that fits in your hand. You can put the pointed stone against the can's top (like a can opener) and hit it with the other stone until the pointed stone punctures the metal surface of the can.

If you look at inventions throughout history, they have been a matter of combining existing notions to create new notions.

The steam train combined notions of a steam engine with a piston and wheels.

The motorcycle combined notions of bicycles and petrol engines.

The car combined notions of petrol engines and carriages. Indeed, early cars were often called "horseless carriages."

Sticky notes, such as Post-It notes combine notions of small pieces of paper and not very sticky glue.

Think about your favourite invention, and you will find it was the result of combining existing notions in a novel way.

DIVERSITY OF NOTIONS = CREATIVITY

This is why dreaming up creative ideas can be difficult for many people. When a person is trying to come up with ideas, her Thought Constructor focuses on notions closely associated with the situation. These notions are stored in proximity in the person's mind and so associate with each other all the time. They naturally come together to form ideas in your mind when you are looking for ideas in a given situation.

To build a creative idea, you need to bring together notions that are not related to the situation into the situation. Combining diverse, seemingly unrelated notions that meet the needs of the situation is the way to build creative ideas.

Think of the classic creativity exercise in which you are asked to come up with as many uses as you possibly can for a commonplace object such as a shoebox. Most people think of boxes as utilities for storing things and will focus their thinking on boxes and storage. A more creative person will associate many more notions to the shoebox, notions such as: weapons (you could hit someone with the box), destruction (you could tear up the shoebox and use the pieces for bookmarks, shopping lists or to fit under the leg of a wobbly table), fires (you could tear up the box to make tinder for a fire), filtering (you could put sandy water in a box; eventually the water will soak through leaving sand in the box) and even kitten transportation (you could put a kitten in the box and slide it across the floor).

This is a critical concept in creativity and ACT: **the creative thinker's creativity comes not from being able to dream up lots of ideas, but from being able to associate many diverse notions to the situation.**

MENTAL BUREAUCRAT

When you are building ideas in your mind, there is another actor, besides the Thought Constructor, that gets involved. It corresponds to a part of the dorsolateral prefrontal region of the brain. In our model of the mind, let us call it the Mental Bureaucrat.

Your Mental Bureaucrat watches and reviews ideas that the Thought Constructor builds and rejects those that it feels are inappropriate. In general, this is a good thing. Your Mental Bureaucrat ensures that you behave properly, in ways that conform to the norms of social behaviour and that your actions are moral, ethical and acceptable. For example, on a hot day, you might briefly be tempted to wear a swimsuit to work. If so, and assuming you are not a lifeguard, the Mental Bureaucrat will reject the idea as inappropriate and prevent you from following through on it.

However, the Mental Bureaucrat can also stifle creativity. This in part because it is often initially difficult to distinguish between a highly creative idea and a stupid idea! So, if you are in a staff meeting when a crazy idea comes to mind, you will probably not be sure if it is a great idea or a stupid one. In order to protect your reputation, your Mental Bureaucrat will assume it is crazy stupid and discourage you from sharing the idea or even thinking too much about it.

However, the Mental Bureaucrat is flexible. In a more relaxed environment, such as the staff canteen over lunch, he may feel that sharing the idea with colleagues is not risky to your reputation. After all, people are often light-hearted at lunch, so if people laugh at your idea it is no big deal.

Over time, most people's Mental Bureaucrats become efficient and effective, ensuring correct behaviour, conforming suitably but not excess-ively to social norms and avoiding saying silly things that might embarrass them – at least most of the time.

However, highly creative people are different as we shall see.

CREATIVE GENIUSES

Interestingly, the minds of highly creative people do two things differently than the minds of people of average creativity. Firstly, the creative individual's Thought Constructor searches more widely in the mind for notions and brings together more diverse notions than the Thought Constructors in others. This diversity of notions results in original ideas.

Secondly, the Mental Bureaucrat in the creative person's mind tends to be less active than the Mental Bureaucrat in the average person's mind, particularly when the creative person is focused on her area of speciality. As a result, crazy ideas are not stopped, but instead they are allowed to grow, get crazier and be shared publicly.

This is why some people find it easy to dream up highly creative ideas while others struggle to have even moderately creative ideas. It is likely also the reason why artists and musicians tend to seem eccentric in behaviour and appearance. Their Mental Bureaucrats do not reject such behaviour as inappropriate.

HOW TO THINK MORE CREATIVELY

Even if you are not a creative genius, there are things you can do to think more creatively. Most of these things focus not so much on having ideas as on getting your Mental Bureaucrat to lighten up and let crazy thinking through.

ALCOHOL

When you have a glass of wine or three (or whatever alcohol you fancy), it also affects your Mental Bureaucrat, causing it to be less scrupulous about filtering thinking. In addition, a relaxed environment – such as your favourite pub or a good friend's sitting room – relaxes the Mental Bureaucrat. As a result, crazier ideas are allowed to pass through. Better still, when fewer ideas are killed, the Thought Constructor probably also lightens up and feels freer to combine diverse, seemingly unrelated notions together to create ideas.

The result, provided you keep your drinking in control, is increased creativity. This is probably why far more creative ideas (in terms of quality and quantity) have been written on beer coasters than on office Post-It notes!

Needless-to-say, you need to be cautious with this approach to creativity enhancement. Firstly, excess alcohol is dangerous to your health. Even small amounts of alcohol are dangerous if you are driving. Drinking and driving is not creative or even clever. It is just bloody stupid! Secondly, as you drink, your creativity might express itself in other ways that are not in your long term interests, for instance: flirting with colleagues, believing you are far funnier than you really are or making rash decisions that seem logical at the time.

Ernest Hemingway is credited with saying, "Write drunk. Edit Sober." And this is good advice in any creative endeavour. If you are having great creative thoughts after a drink or three – document them thoroughly. But review them and act on them only when you have sobered up!

WANDERING MIND

One of my favourite ways to have ideas is to let my mind wander to wherever it may go. When the mind wanders, the Mental Bureaucrat also relaxes and allows crazier ideas to get through than normal. This is why people tend to have their best ideas when going for a walk, taking a bath or doing other relaxing, unfocused activities. These activities allow the mind to wander while allowing the body to relax.

I personally find walking and, to a lesser extent, riding on trains ideal times for creative thinking. The passing scenery inspires creative thinking; movement inspires me, and my mind loves to wander.

Where do you have your best ideas? Wherever it is, it is the place where your mind feels freest to wander and where your Mental Bureaucrat feels it can rest a bit and not watch your thoughts so carefully.

RANDOM INFORMATION

Probably the most useful quick and easy creativity trick is to bring some kind of random information into your understanding of a situation. You can do this by opening a book and choosing a random word; by asking how a person or organisation completely different to yours would handle the situation; or by comparing the situation to a completely different situation that has no obvious relevance to yours.

This forces the mind to bring together seemingly unrelated notions that can result in surprisingly creative ideas. However, you need to be sure that the Mental Bureaucrat allows those ideas to form in your mind and be shared with others.

ANTICONVENTIONAL THINKING

ACT is the result of my goal to design a creative thinking process around the way the mind generates and filters creative ideas. While designing the process, it became clear that it would need to accomplish two things.

Firstly, it would need to push the Thought Constructor to put together more diverse notions that would normally be the case; combinations of notions that would seem unconventional, but which make sense.

Secondly, ACT would need temporarily to reprogramme the Mental Bureaucrat to reject conventional ideas in favour of unconventional ideas. But only temporarily.

Hence the name and concept. Anticonventional thinking = purposefully rejecting conventional ideas in favour of unconventional ideas when you want to be creative.

Now, let us see how ACT works, but before we can do that, we need to think about situations in which we want to be creative. After all, most of us neither want nor need to be creative all the time. It would be exhausting.

TRANSCENDENTAL SITUATIONS

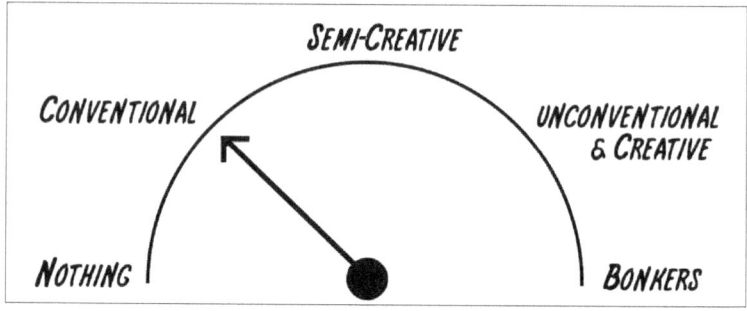

NOT ALL SITUATIONS REQUIRE CREATIVE ACTION

In any given situation, you have a choice of actions you can take, from doing nothing to doing something conventional, to doing something insane. In most situations, there is no need to think through the options; you can and should do the conventional thing.

However, in those situations where you want to do something creative, you should consider the options available. These options typically span a conceptual spectrum.

DO NOTHING

In some situations, you may simply decide to do nothing. That is okay. Often, doing nothing is the most sensible action you can take in a situation.

In other situations, however, you may be so overwhelmed by options that you do not make a choice and do nothing by default. In other situations, you may choose to do something very creative, but when it comes time to take action, you feel intimidated by your crazy-creative idea and fail to do anything.

These latter scenarios are often not okay, and we will address them in the ACT process.

Do the Conventional Thing

In most situations, you (like most people) probably do the conventional thing without thinking about it. Indeed, the only time the average person tends to think about the conventional thing is when she is not sure what the conventional action is in a given situation. Fortunately, Google and other search engines have made it easy to identify the conventional action in any situation.

Conventional action is usually, though not always, the safest action to take in a situation. Conventionality makes it unlikely that the action is socially, morally or legally unacceptable. However, this is not always true. Repression of a particular group of people in a society may be conventional in that society, but it is ethically wrong.

Do Something Semi-Creative

Sometimes, you do not want to do the conventional thing, and you look for alternatives. Perhaps you spend some time on Google looking for less conventional actions to take in a particular situation. Perhaps you are inspired by a creative person or someone from another culture whose conventions are different to yours.

In such a situation, you action is not truly creative; you did not build it in your own mind. Rather, you were inspired to take an action similar to that taken by another person. However, the action you take is different to you.

Doing something semi-creative is better than it may sound. The very nature of taking an action that is new and unconventional to you opens the mind and helps you see less conventional actions you can take in other situations. It also provides your mind with new notions and connections that can be used in building creative ideas for the current situation or future situations.

Do Something Creative

Sometimes you want or need to do something original. Instead of looking for actions to copy, you devise your own unconventional, original, creative action to take.

Creative action can often be the most challenging action to take. You need to dream up a creative idea; you need to go against convention and you may be taking risks. Creative action is by its very nature new and untested. It may not work. But it probably will.

Do Something Bonkers

Sometimes, because a person is insane, very drunk, under the influence of drugs or for other reasons is not acting rationally, she may choose to do something that is irrelevant to the situation. It is not a rational choice. It does not make sense. Nevertheless, it happens.

Sometimes, when you are trying to be creative, you may worry that an idea is bonkers and be tempted to reject it rather than play with it. However, unless you are heavily under the influence of drink or drugs; or you have a history of serious mental health problems, that seemingly bonkers idea is probably a creative idea. So, don't worry about it. Play with it instead.

TRANSCENDENTAL SITUATIONS

If you decide not to do the conventional thing, but to seek a creative action to take in a situation, we call it a "transcendental situation" because the situation transcends ordinary situations and becomes special. A transcendental situation is one in which you stop and think. You look at the options and then use your mind to try to build a creative vision of an action you could take.

Whether or not you eventually decide to take creative action matters not. The fact that you are thinking about the situation in some depth and considering creative action makes it transcendental.

In the next two chapters, we'll look at example transcendental situations and the various options they present.

A Story: Transcendental Holidays

John is a middle manager in a software company based near London. Every year, for holiday, he spends two weeks in St Malo, a lovely walled city on the coast of France. He stays in his favourite hotel, relaxes on the beach and enjoys the excellent seafood and wine on offer. He has a few friends who either live there or travel there regularly. He has got his favourite nightspots and inevitably has a good time. Because it is familiar, he also finds it a low-stress holiday, which he appreciates as his job can sometimes be stressful.

That has been particularly true of late. There have been rumours about a merger and everyone knows that these days a merger usually leads to a loss of jobs.

As it happened, the rumours were true, and his company has been bought out by a big American firm. This is good news for John; he owned a small piece of the company and so has made a big chunk of money as a result of the buy-out. Better still, he received a promotion and a generous pay rise.

John is delighted by the outcome and his new found wealth. When it comes time to plan his holiday, he decides to look at some alternatives to his usual trip. After all, he is wealthier than he was a few months ago and has a promotion to celebrate. He starts researching his options.

This story has four possible endings.

ENDING ONE: NO ACTION

John searches the web, buys travel guides and talks to friends who give him all kinds of varied advice. John becomes so overwhelmed by options that he cannot make a decision and does not take a trip this year.

ENDING TWO: CONVENTIONAL ACTION

After spending a couple of evenings researching the options, John feels none of them would be as nice as his usual trip to St Malo. One of the reasons he likes his regular annual holiday is because he does not need to make any decisions or risk any uncertainty. He can relax and enjoy himself in familiar surroundings and know that he will have a good time.

He books his usual trip and looks forward to it.

ENDING THREE: SEMI-CREATIVE ACTION

Reading the Sunday newspaper, John sees an article about hiking in Myanmar (Burma) that includes some inspiring pictures. At the end of the article are some websites that he visits. He discovers a fascinating package tour that includes a guide, special hikes, accommodation and more. He promptly books his trip and looks forward to something different. And because it is an organised trip, he knows he can relax and not worry about the details.

This choice is something that is new and different for John, and it is likely to inspire him. But it is not an original idea. Rather it is an unusual idea that he found in his research. So, it is a semi-creative action.

ENDING FOUR: CREATIVE ACTION

John has always enjoyed American road films and loves the idea of big cars and exploring the West. He finds a car rental company that has classic American convertibles available and books a massive Cadillac. He spends time poring over maps and guidebooks in order to find stunning spots in the West. He maps out a trip, books a few hotels and decides to leave some places to chance. He books his flight, spends three weeks exploring the American West in a big Cadillac convertible and has the time of his life.

This is a truly creative solution for John. He has put the trip together in his mind by combining notions about the Western USA, old cars and driving. He finds more information – that becomes notions for building his vision. The trip is the result of his creative vision building.

Of course, others have done similar trips. On a global level, his decision is not that creative. But from his perspective and the perspective of his friends it is creative.

ENDING FIVE: BONKERS ACTION

The recent stress at work has proven too much for John. For reasons no one understands, he now likes to dress up in a felt rabbit costume and hop around the streets of London, reciting Shakespeare's sonnets.

John's final choice of action is not the result of sound judgement or rational creativity, rather it is the act of a snapped mind. His actions bear no resemblance to the situation or his goals.

IT'S ALL IN THE MIND

Creativity takes place in the mind. Making a situation transcendental does not mean that the action you will take is necessarily creative. It simply means that you are exploring creative ideas and building creative visions.

In John's story, the situation became transcendental once he decided to explore his options. Consider another possible ending to the story.

ENDING SIX: MIND CHANGE

As in ending four, John starts researching a trip to America, he looks into hiring a Cadillac convertible and examines maps of the West. It is a compelling choice. But he eventually decides it would be too complicated to arrange, and he starts feeling a little apprehensive about going to America. He envisions things going wrong, trouble with visas, being held-up at gunpoint, having an accident in the desert. After much thought, he decides to take the conventional choice and books his usual trip to St Malo – or he simply does not book a holiday at all.

TOO COMMONPLACE

Unfortunately, I see Ending Six (Mind Change) happening frequently, especially in business. Ideas are captured in idea management systems and brainstorms. Visions are developed in anticonventional thinking (ACT) sessions. Great concepts are scribbled down on the back of beer coasters at the pub around the corner from the office.

But when the owners of the ideas, visions or concepts get back to their desks and their daily routines, they lose interest and motivation to pursue their ideas. As a result, nothing happens.

Perhaps the idea is too risky. Perhaps the participants are too busy with other tasks. For whatever reason, nothing happens. We will look at how to implement ideas later in this book. For now, the thing to bear in mind is that transcendental situations can, and often do, result in creative thinking but no action.

This is why it is a good idea in any transcendental situation to ask yourself what would happen if you did nothing or if you took the conventional action. In business, if your competitors are innovating their products, while you do nothing or keep doing the same thing, you give your competitors a chance to outdo you and very likely steal sales from you.

Brigit shared a picture

Trying on new blouse at Kwerps. What do you think? :-)

Jeffrey Baumgartner and 58 others like this

Beautiful! Buy it!

A BUSINESS STORY: E-SHOPPING

Jessica is the senior marketing manager at Kwerps, a fast-growing chain of trendy clothing boutiques. She has been put in charge of the current website, which is presently no more than a promotional tool with shop information, nice pictures, announcements of sales and that kind of thing.

Her job is to update the website, include on-line shopping elements, exploit social media and drive a significant percentage of sales through the web within two years.

The situation is clearly a transcendental one. She needs to take action. She wants to take creative action. Let's look at the options.

ENDING ONE: DO NOTHING

Jessica could, of course, opt to do nothing. She calls a lot of meetings, discusses the situation to death, does some research, holds more meetings and ultimately fails to change the web presence at all. Fortunately, Jessica is adept at company politics and blames Harold, an irritating colleague, for her failure to take any real action.

ENDING TWO: CONVENTIONAL ACTION

Jessica looks at what Kwerps's competitors are doing and makes a list of the features she likes. She then hires a web development team to create an on-line shop following best practice. The Kwerps.com home page displays a very good looking model wearing Kwerps clothes. Products are categorised, and shoppers can click on links to see tops, trousers, accessories, special offers and so on. Smaller links, at the bottom of the page, lead to corporate information, job opportunities and that kind of thing.

Oh, and since social media is de rigueur these days, Jessica sets up Facebook, Google Plus and Twitter accounts that promote special offers, competitions and company news. On Twitter, she exchanges occasional twitteresque comments with cool people who follow Kwerps. She pays some of those people to follow her company.

It all looks good and soon generates on-line sales. They are not spectacular sales, but the results are not bad either.

This is often the case with conventional action. It is not creative, but it is not risky. Results are usually predictable and seldom spectacular.

ENDING THREE: SEMI-CREATIVE ACTION

While researching, Jessica discovers a Milan-based men's clothing e-shop with a very stylish web presentation and some interesting features – like answering customers' questions about fashion, recommending accessories and colour matching – that Jessica likes. Moreover, the Milan-based e-shop is limited to the Italian language, so it will be unfamiliar to the English- speaking market she targets.

Jessica shows the Italian website to the web team and, being fluent in Italian herself, she is able to explain the features. They discuss what they like and do not like about the Milan e-shop and then build a Kwerps e-shop inspired by the Milan e-shop.

This ending is semi-creative. Jessica has looked for an unusual approach, but rather than develop ideas on her own or with her team, she looked for an unusual mod-

el and used that as the basis for Kwerps's e-shop.

ENDING FOUR: CREATIVE ACTION

Jessica thinks long and hard about shopping on-line and in real-world shops. She talks to a lot of her friends and chats with customers in Kwerps shops. One thing she notices is that many people – women in particular – see real-world shopping as a social activity. Sweethearts go shopping together. Women often go shopping with friends. But unless two people share a computer, they cannot easily go shopping on-line together.

She also observes that people often research what is available on-line, but go to the shops to try items on. Yet, there are few linkages between on-line and off-line shopping.

A vision is beginning to form in Jessica's creative mind.

She begins to explore ways that two or more people could shop on-line together while actually being physically apart and using different devices. Ideas include a space for chat, talking, sharing pages and video communication. Shoppers would be able to show potential purchases to friends and ask for their thoughts. Jessica envisages an on-line "coffee shop" for the shoppers to stop, have a coffee and talk over a video link.

Friends e-shopping together will be able to look at each other's shopping baskets and see which products their friends are visiting. They can like things and give feedback. Nevertheless, either shopper can also secretly add items to her cart if she does not want her friend to see.

Jessica then starts to think about how to combine on-line shopping with real-world shopping. She imagines someone in a bricks and mortar shop photographing items using a smartphone – or an in-shop photo-booth with nice lighting and backgrounds – and sharing images with friends on social networks such as Facebook and Twitter. People could even opt to show off, on the Kwerps Facebook page, clothes they try on. This, Jessica realises, will be great for connecting with their customers.

Over time and sharing thoughts with colleagues and friends, Jessica soon develops a comprehensive creative vision of how the Kwerps.com on-line shopping experience would feel and how it could link with off-line shopping.

This is truly creative action. Jessica and her team have combined a lot of existing ideas about shopping and sharing a creative vision that stands out from the competition's on-line activities. They are sure to make news.

ENDING FIVE: BONKERS ACTION

Work stress becomes too much for Jessica, who comes from a family with a history of schizophrenia. She starts having mental health issues, which her superiors fail to detect in their determination to work her as hard as possible.

She decides to replace the entire existing website with a collection of cute cat videos which she insists are far more interesting than fashion. She even goes so far as to build a prototype.

Jessica is not thinking rationally and while she deserves sympathy, her creative vision clearly has no connection to reality or the situation for which she was looking for ideas.

LATENT AND ACTIVE SITUATIONS

So far, we have been looking at active, transcendental situations in which you are trying to build a creative vision. The situation has been in your mind, and you have been deep-viewing it. However, from time to time, a brilliant idea pops into your head for no apparent reason. You are not focusing on a situation relevant to the idea. But the idea invades your mind nonetheless.

In this case, the idea responds not to an active transcendental situation that you are reflecting on now, but rather a latent situation; a situation that you have thought about in the past and which sits in the back of your mind even though you do not realise it is there.

Cathy is a senior designer for a large furniture manufacturer. For the past year and a half she has been responsible for dining room pieces. She has done well. Her Mediterranean inspired sets have been particularly popular.

One evening, she sits down on her sofa, with a laptop on her lap and her smartphone on the arm of the sofa, to watch TV, catch up on personal email and hopefully exchange some SMSs with her boyfriend who is away on a business trip. While she is juggling these devices – not to mention a glass of Merlot on the coffee table – she is suddenly inspired. Wouldn't it be great, she thinks, to have a sofa with a retractable table that can be stowed away in the arm? It would be specially designed to hold a laptop or tablet. It would be tilt-able but have a rimmed edge to prevent things from sliding off. The side of the sofa could even have electrical points for plugging in electrical devices. Of course, the table would not be limited to electronic devices. It could also be used for setting down a book or anything else. She fetches her notebook and makes a number of quick sketches. Tomorrow, she will send them to Jan, who is responsible for this kind of thing.

Cathy, of course, is not actively thinking about designing sofas – it is not her job these days. But she is a designer, she has worked on such furniture in the past and she has opened her mind to inspiration for furniture design. As a result, the design of furniture and other things not a part of dining room furniture, is a latent situation. She has thought about these things in the past; she is always looking for inspiration, and she can be inspired with ideas and visions that respond to this latent situation.

THE METHOD

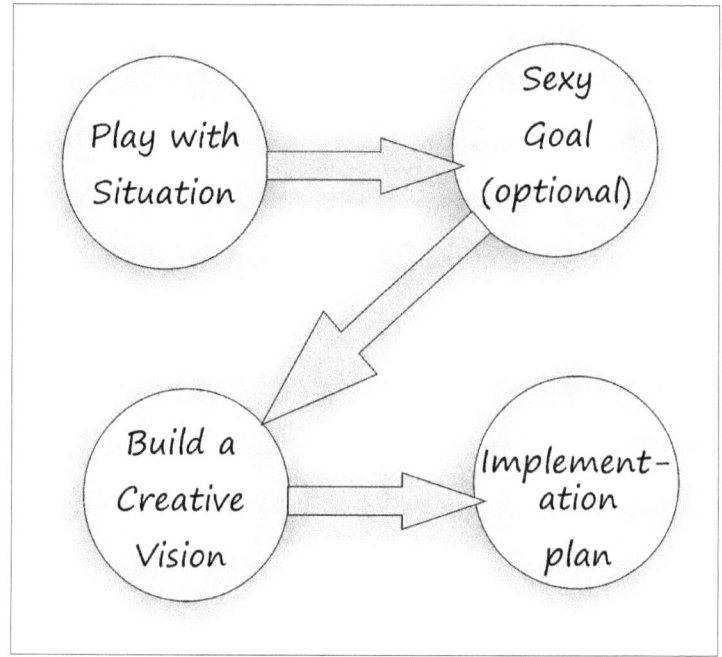

A FOUR STEP PROCESS

ACT can be broken down into a simple three or four step process depending on whether you are working alone, in a small group or with a larger group.

1. Play with the situation.

2. Develop a sexy goal (Optional).

3. Build a creative vision.

4. Build an implementation plan.

In the next chapters, we will look in detail at each of the steps in the ACT process.

STEP 1: PLAY WITH THE SITUATION

When you have a transcendental situation – in other words, a situation in which you have decided to consider taking unconventional, creative action – your first instinct may very well be to try to generate ideas. This is a normal feeling. But it is wrong. In fact, you should spend time playing with the situation so that you can look at it from various perspectives, understand its fundamental nature better and connect seemingly unrelated notions to the situation in order to see what happens.

Why is it wrong to generate ideas right away?

The answer is simple. When you first confront a transcendental situation, you normally only perceive the surface, usually in the form of a simple verbal description or visual image of the situation, which limits the number and diversity of notions you associate with the situation. Now, as I trust you recall, creative ideas are formed by connecting notions together to create all new notions. If you cannot connect many notions to the situation and those notions are not very diverse, it is clearly not going to be easy to come up with creative ideas.

On the other hand, if you look deep into a situation; if you look at a situation from various perspectives; if you associate all kinds of seemingly unconnected notions with a situation, then it is remarkably easy to come up with creative ideas. And the best way to do all these things with a situation is to play with it.

There are four ways you can play with a situation.

1. Meditation

2. Questions

3. Mind-Wandering

4. Mental Fermentation

We will look at each of these ways in the next chapters of this book, but first two words of advice.

WORD OF ADVICE 1: MISUNDERSTANDING A SITUATION

Being too quick to have ideas, rather than understand a situation, not only makes it difficult to have truly creative ideas, it also makes it all too likely that you misunderstand the situation and, as a result, build ideas that do not truly address the situation or which make the situation worse.

Anika sees a baby in a pushchair outside a bakery. The baby is crying, and there is a milk bottle laying on the ground next to the pushchair. Anika picks up the milk bottle and hands it to the baby who looks at it, flings it to the ground and continues crying – even louder. Anika laughs, picks up the bottle and soothingly encourages the baby to take the bottle and drink from it.

"What are you doing to my baby?" asks a shocked woman who has run out from the bakery. "And why are you trying to force your bottle onto her?"

Of course, Anika assumed the bottle belonged to the baby, that he was crying because he was hungry and that he had dropped the bottle. In fact, the bottle belonged to another baby who had been parked outside the bakery an hour ago while her mother was buying bread.

Not surprisingly, the mother was shocked to see Anika trying to push a strange bottle on her baby. And Anika felt awful. She had seen a situation and tried to help the baby. But by misunderstanding it, she actually made the situation worse.

In the story, Anika completely misunderstood a situation and took action that was inappropriate and made the situation worse. This frequently happens when people are too quick to try and have ideas: they misunderstand the very nature of a transcendental situation and their ideas either do nothing or make a situation worse.

WORD OF ADVICE 2: TAKE NOTES

Before we dive into the various methods of playing with situations in order to understand them better and deeper, there is one absolutely critical thing you must be prepared to do: take notes!

Playing with a situation should inspire you with insights and inspirations. But much of that inspiration will not come in useful until the third phase: that of building a creative vision. So, be absolutely sure that you have a notebook or a laptop or a smartphone available for note taking. The device does not matter as long as you are comfortable using it.

I am a traditionalist in this sense and always carry a small Moleskin or similar sized notebook with me. It fits conveniently in a pocket, allows me to write notes or draw, and it is not reliant on batteries. However, use what works for you. The device is not important. The ability to take and return to notes is critical.

This is probably the single most important bit of creativity advice you will get in this or any other creative thinking book!

Now, let us look at how you can play with transcendental situations.

"Oh, don't worry. That's just Patricia's way to
reflect on product development."

MEDITATION – COSMIC CREATIVITY

Cosmic creativity, or inner-mind creativity is a variation on meditation
where you go deep into your inner mind in order to explore and play with
a situation. It takes elements of meditation as used in Theravada
Buddhism combined with visualisation techniques. It is not difficult, and
if you are familiar with meditation, you can do Cosmic Creativity.

Before we dive into the process, we need to talk about your inner
mind. If you were to visit your inner mind, walk around and explore it,
what would it look like? A house? A field? A forest? A flower? Deep
space? There is no correct answer. In my workshops, I have heard all of
these and more. What is important is that you have a vision of your inner
mind for meditation.

GUIDED MEDITATION

When I lead a Cosmic Creativity meditation session, we start with simple
stretching exercises followed by a discussion about transcendental situations. Then we talk about the inner mind and each participant is asked to
think about and visualise her inner mind.

When everyone is ready, I lead the group through breathing and re-
laxation exercises to calm their minds and then I lead them into a

meditative state in which each individual walks through her mind until she comes to her transcendental situation.

Participants first look at their situations, then walk around and within them. They fly overhead. They shrink the situation and enlarge it. I introduce random objects, people and animals to the situation.

After playing with the situation in a variety of ways, participants are given time to explore their situations on their own before leaving the meditative state. They are then given some quiet time to take notes and reflect on the experience.

After such sessions, I am always amazed at the number of people who come to me telling me of the insights Cosmic Creativity has given them. Indeed, people sometimes find solutions to their problems that have eluded them for a long time, particularly if the situation is not a complex one. In this case, the people in question are ready to move on to the vision building step of ACT.

SELF-INDUCED MEDITATION

It is not always possible to have a coach put you into a meditative state. Fortunately, it is possible to put yourself into a meditative state. I have summarised the method below. However, if you have the opportunity to learn how to meditate through a coach or a workshop, I suggest you take advantage of the opportunity. Meditation is a useful skill; one I learned about from Buddhist monks while living in Southeast Asia in the late 1980s and the 1990s.

Here is a short and simplified method to put yourself in a relaxed, meditative state and to ponder your situation. Give it a go!

1. Find a quiet and comfortable space where you will not be disturbed.

2. If this is your first time, take a few moments to think about your inner mind and visualise it as a place where you could walk around.

3. Get into a relaxed position, such as sitting or laying down.

4. Focus on your breathing.

5. Take slow, deep breaths.

6. Visualise the top of your head and consciously relax it.

7. Continue this process down your body. Visualise segments of your body, your forehead, your eyes, your nose and ears and so on, relaxing each bit as you move downwards until you have relaxed your toes. With each exhalation, feel the stress leaving your body like waves of tension flowing into the floor.

8. Continue this process until your body is relaxed, and the only sound is your breathing.

9. Imagine yourself in your inner mind – the mind we spoke about a while ago. What does it look like? What does it feel like? Make yourself comfortable, you will be spending some time here. If you are not happy with your mind, change it and start this exercise again. Fortunately, it is your mind, and you can change it!

10. Once you are comfortable in your mind, begin walking in your mind until you approach your situation..

11. Think about how this situation came to be. Why does it exist?

12. In your mind, walk around the situation. Look at it from various angles. What do you see? What do you feel? What do you hear? What do you smell?

13. Fly above and below the situation. What do you see?

14. Are other people involved in the situation? What are they doing? How do they perceive the situation? What would they like you to do? How might they be affected by your creative action?

15. Change the colour of the situation. Make it red or green or blue. The colour does not matter. How does the situation look and feel now?

16. Change the colour again.

17. Let the situation return to its natural colours.

18. Does the situation remind you in any way of other, seemingly different situations? How do the situations compare? How do they differ?

19. Let animals, such as cats, dogs, penguins, horses or any other species enter your situation and explore it.

20. Bring random people or objects into the situation and see what

happens. (If you are meditating alone, before you start, choose a few random words from the dictionary or images from a picture book and keep them in mind for your meditation.)

21. Continue to explore your situation until you are ready to re-enter the material world.

22. Once you have returned to the material world, write down your insights in a notebook, on a tablet or whatever works for you. Keep the notebook nearby for 24 hours. You will often find inspiration continues to come long after the meditation.

WALKING MEDITATION

Meditation need not be sitting still in a quiet space. You can and should try walking meditation. Although you obviously cannot get into such a deep meditative state while walking, walking does have the advantage of being exercise, exposing you to ever-changing inspiration in the form of scenery and providing movement which, I find, helps one to think.

I prefer walking self-meditation over the sitting kind. I find it helps me explore situations more comprehensively. However, one needs to be careful. I was once so absorbed in thought, while on a walk, that I walked into a signpost and broke my nose. Really!

OTHER FORMS OF MEDITATION

You can meditate in all kinds of ways as long as those ways themselves do not require much thinking. For instance, driving a car and meditating would not be a good idea!

However, some people meditate in the bathtub – even having special candles for meditation. Others find a quiet place in a forest, atop a mountain or in a coffee shop in which to reflect.

If you find a place or a way in which you feel comfortable and able to zone out of the local reality in order to enter the reality of your mind, then the place is perfect for your meditation.

ASKING QUESTIONS

In addition to meditation, asking questions is a powerful way to see a situation from various perspectives particularly if you are working with a team of people. Questions and answers help the entire team explore a situation in depth together.

There are three kinds of questions to be used in ACT:

1.   Analytical questions.

2.   Feeling questions.

3.   Transcendental questions.

In a business context, or if you are familiar with creative problem-solving (CPS), you will be most familiar with analytical questions. They are the norm and are essential for being sure you understand the nature of the situation. However, analytical questions fail to dig deep into situations in order to really understand them; nor do they encourage anticonventional thinking. Analytical questions provide a good, analytical understanding of a situation and are particularly useful for ensuring that you understand the situation correctly, which is critical. Misunderstanding a transcendental situation, as we shall see, at best, leads to creative visions that fail to do what you want to do and, at worst, has serious consequences.

Analytical Questions

As the name implies, analytical questions enable you to analyse a situation in a rational manner. The best analytical question to start with is actually a set of five questions to be asked in sequence: the five whys. As its name implies, the five whys is asking why a situation exists five times in order to drill down and identify the core elements of a situation. This is important because people often only see the surface of a situation and perhaps fail to understand its true nature. The five whys helps you dig down to the truth.

Here is a rather sad story about someone who should have asked the five whys of himself.

Marvin's Misunderstanding

Marvin is an intelligent young man with a wife, two kids and a promising, highly paid job in a major multinational company. His wife is a teacher who enjoys her job, but does not bring in a lot of income.

A vice president of the company is leaving, and Marvin reckons he has an excellent chance to get the post. It would mean more work and a lot of travel. In exchange, he would get a big salary increase, performance bonuses and stock options.

Marvin goes all out to indicate his interest in the post and impress the CEO and other top managers. This takes up a lot of time, but eventually he wins the promotion. As expected, he is soon staying late at the office, travelling regularly and on those weekends he is not travelling, he often spends time on his laptop catching up on important emails.

On a plus side, he is raking in money, plans to buy a grand house soon and is often buying his family gifts.

Within two years, Marvin's wife divorces him and eventually moves in with George, a musician who lives in a small house and seems always to be struggling for money. Sadly, from Martin's perspective, his kids also seem really happy with George, who can often be seen playing with them in the garden of the small house.

Marvin hopes to have some free time early next month, when there are no business trips planned, to play with his children too. But he might have to go to Singapore for a really important meeting.

As you have doubtless worked out, Marvin misunderstood his situation. He thought it was that he needed money to provide materially for his family and in his pursuit of earning more money, he ended up neglecting his family emotionally and physically.

If only Marvin's best friend, David, had asked Marvin the Five Whys and perhaps a few other questions.

Marvin: *I need to win the post of vice president at work.*

David: *Why do you need to do that?*

Marvin: *Because it will mean a lot more money.*

David: *Why do you need a lot more money?*

Marvin: *Because I want to provide for my family.*

David: *Why do you want to provide for your family?*

Marvin: *Because I love them and want them to have everything they desire.*

David: *Why do you need more money to love them and give them everything they desire.*

Marvin: *Because, without money, I cannot buy them the best of everything.*

David: *Why is that important?*

Marvin: *Because I love them!*

The two men pause and think for a moment ...

David: *The situation as I see it is that you love your family and want to provide for them.*

Marvin: *Yes, that's what I have just said!*

David: *But are you sure that more money is the only way to express that? How else could you love and provide for them?*

Marvin: *Well ... By spending more time with them. By holding them. By helping them with problems. By playing with them.*

David: *That sounds like the kind of things your wife and kids need. Would getting that promotion help you do those things?*

Marvin: *No, it would make it harder to do those things. I'd be away a lot. But the money would be great!*
David: *How?*

Marvin: *We could buy a bigger house, nicer clothes, take nice vacations ...*

David: *Has your family expressed a desire for these things?*

Marvin: *Now that you mention it, no they haven't.*

David: *Do you think those things are more important than time, affection, helping them with problems and playing with them? Because it seems to me that you effectively have to choose one or the other.*

Marvin: *I need to think about that!*

The five whys is a powerful set of questions. In my workshops, participants are often surprised at what they learn through this technique.

There is no need to stop with the five whys. Other analytical questions you can ask include ...

- What has caused this situation to occur?

- Who is affected by the situation?

- What are the constraints we face in implementing a solution?

- Do our competitors face similar situations? If so, how are they responding?

- How would we like the situation to be in one year? In five years?

- What are the consequences of doing nothing in the situation?

- What would be the conventional thing to do in this situation? Why do we not want to take this action?

- Who needs to approve our solution?

Feeling Questions

Feeling questions enable you to understand the emotions of all involved; something that is often not addressed in business innovation with its focus on analysis. But understanding these feelings is critical in terms of understanding a situation as well as seeing the situation from new perspectives. Feeling questions include:

- How do we feel about this situation?

- How would we like to feel?

- How do our customers feel?

- Are there other people involved in the situation? How do they feel about it?

- How would we like them to feel about our creative action?

- How do the relevant decision makers feel about the situation, eventual actions we might take and the potential risks?

It is usually a good idea to ask, "why" after each of these questions in order to elaborate upon the answer. Also ask whether you know how someone feels, or you are only guessing how they feel. If the latter, on what do you base your judgement? If you are passionate about a new product your company is launching, you may believe that your customers are also passionate about the product when they may only be mildly interested.

Feeling questions might, for example, indicate that while a plan to automate customer service processes is a winner from a cost-savings and efficiency perspective, implementation of the plan will almost certainly cause a lot of unhappiness among staff affected by the change as well as customers used to human interaction with your company.

Indeed, any big business change is likely to cause feelings of uncertainty, which will make it harder to win people over to your creative vision. Addressing feelings while analysing a transcendental situation ensures you also address them when building a vision of the action you will take in the situation.

TRANSCENDENTAL QUESTIONS

Transcendental questions are great fun and enable you to see a transcendental situation in new ways. They also enable your mind to build connections between the transcendental situation and other information, thoughts and situations. These connections make developing ideas into truly creative visions much easier!

Transcendental questions are questions that seem a little absurd, but bring insight into a situation; they can include questions such as these.

- What colour is the situation?

- What would happen if you painted the situation blue? Red?

- What would happen if we introduced a group of cats and dogs into the situation?

- What would McDonalds (the fast food chain) do in a situation like this?

- How does the situation feel about itself? Why?

- How does the situation smell? Why?

- What would your grandmother do in this situation?

- What outcome would the situation itself prefer? Why?

- Use your favourite meal as a metaphor for the situation and then describe the situation in that context.

- If you could shrink the situation so that it fit into your hand, how would it look? How would it feel?

- How would the situation solve itself?

- What animal most closely resembles your situation?

- What are the three most interesting aspects of your situation?

Warning: asking and answer transcendental questions may lead to laughter and less than serious answers. Do not panic. This is a good thing! It means that people are relaxing, letting their guards down and, as a result, putting themselves in an optimal frame of mind for creativity!

Transcendental questions may seem irreverent, but they are very powerful because they force your mind to look at the situation in new ways that, in turn, associates unexpected notions with the situation. Such notions are the very food of creative thought and make it easier to build unconventional, creative ideas.

DANCE

Believe it or not, dance – or at least movement and gesture inspired by dance – is a great way to analyse a situation, especially one that involves multiple people who may have conflicting motivations in the situation. This is a relatively new approach I've been developing together with dance instructor, coach and friend, Elena Leibbrand. We call it, "human dynamic problem solving" (HDPS) because it can actually be used as an entire problem-solving method, though its main function is more of a problem or situation analysis tool.

You should have a dance instructor or coach involved in the facilitation of the workshop or at least someone familiar with dance.

BEFORE YOU START

It is critical to do the HDPS workshop outside of the office. HDPS involves participants relaxing, moving and doing things not very office-like. Even moderately self-conscious people will feel uncomfortable doing such things in the office, especially if their colleagues, who are not participating in the HDPS activity, might see them.

I prefer to run HDPS workshops with groups that can be divided into at least two teams, each with about five people and each team doing a choreography, so that there is always an audience to watch each team's performance and provide feedback. Comparing audience feedback to participant feedback is lightening as we will see in the example below.

How HDPS Works

The first step is to perform warm up exercises to relax participants and introduce them into the language of dance and movement. Eventually, the warm up exercises should move from warming up to impersonating moods, actions and even inanimate objects such as photocopiers or chairs. This opens participants' minds to thinking about how to present ideas with their bodies.

One member of the group explains the situation to the others (if they are not already familiar with it). The others then ask questions about the situation to understand it.

This done, the team members take roles in the situation and work together to design a short choreography in which they impersonate the situation using gesture, movement and meaningless sounds. Dialogue and explanation are not permitted.

Once they are ready, each team performs its choreography in front of the others. Once they have completed it, the facilitator leads a question session in which she asks each performer as well as the audience questions with a focus on feelings, motivations and personal perspective. What you will often find is different people interpret the situation differently and even ascribe different feelings to the same performer. As a result, HDPS can be a real eye-opener in terms of understanding how conflicting and complementary feelings and motivations can affect a situation.

Let us see how it works in an example.

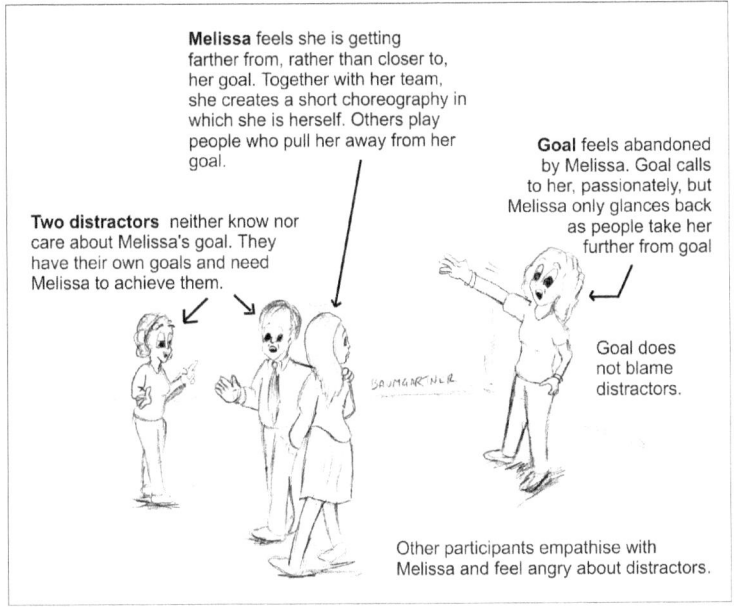

Melissa feels she is getting farther from, rather than closer to, her goal. Together with her team, she creates a short choreography in which she is herself. Others play people who pull her away from her goal.

Goal feels abandoned by Melissa. Goal calls to her, passionately, but Melissa only glances back as people take her further from goal

Two distractors neither know nor care about Melissa's goal. They have their own goals and need Melissa to achieve them.

Goal does not blame distractors.

Other participants empathise with Melissa and feel angry about distractors.

MELISSA'S MISSING GOAL

Three groups of people participate in a HDPS workshop to solve work related personal problems. The workshop is facilitated by Jeremy, an ACT facilitator, and Edna, a dance coach.

After Jeremy's short introduction, Edna leads the group through some warm up exercises that involve moving their bodies and making gestures to impersonate a wide range of things, from themselves being angry to being a photocopier or a jammed printer.

Jeremy follows with a short talk about problems, accepting personal responsibility for them and the need to play a role in solving the problem.

The facilitators invite three people to share problems. Teams of five are formed around each problem, and each team is instructed to use the language of movement, as they had practised earlier, to create a short choreography about their problem. They are not allowed to use spoken word, though noises are allowed. Teams each find a quiet place to work. After the problem, owners explain their problems in more detail, their team-mates ask questions for clarification. The teams then collaborate in designing their choreographies. The facilitators coach the teams as they develop their choreograph-

ies.

Let's look at the problem and choreography of one of the participants, Melissa. She has been feeling frustrated because although she is advancing in her career, she is moving away from her own professional goals.

In Melissa's group's choreography, one woman plays the goal. She stays in the far corner of the room throughout. Initially, Melissa (playing herself) stands near to her goal, but soon she starts moving away towards Nicholas who gently takes her arm and walks her away from the goal, gesturing as if he has an important task for her. As Melissa walks away, the goal gestures and makes noises to get Melissa's attention, which Melissa largely ignores. Nicholas pays it no attention whatsoever and does not even look at the animated goal.

Then Olivia takes Melissa's other arm and pulls her away from Nicholas, leading her further away from the goal. At the same time, the goal becomes more frantic in trying to get Melissa's attention, making desperate sounds, jumping and waving wildly from her spot in the corner of the room. Melissa pays her goal even less attention and focuses on Olivia.

At the end of the choreography, Melissa has been led out of the workshop room and is looking sadly back in where she can see her goal sadly looking back at her. It was a very touching and powerful performance from a group of professional people with no formal training in dance or theatre. It was also very insightful.

At the end of the choreography, the facilitator leads a discussion about the team's performance, and there are a few surprises. Many in the audience identify with Melissa's situation and several even feel anger towards Nicholas and Olivia for taking Melissa away from her goal. Many ask why the goal did not move towards Melissa, which is a good question, and one we will address in a moment.

Interestingly, the goal said that she did not feel any anger towards Nicholas or Olivia. She felt mostly frustrated and sad that she was being ignored. Neither Nicholas nor Olivia had any feelings towards Melissa's goal or Melissa's desire to go closer to it. They had their own agendas and required Melissa's help to get there. That they pulled Melissa from her own goal was of no interest to them.

Melissa felt mostly frustration with herself, which was also evident in her choreography, though she also blamed Nicholas and Olivia for preventing her from achieving her goal.

Although Melissa's problem seems a relatively simple one on the surface, the choreography demonstrates the hidden complexity when people with different motivations are working together but not necessarily towards common goals. Giving Melissa's goal emotions was interesting because it had slightly different feelings than Melissa and demonstrated a more honest observation of the situation. While Melissa partially blamed, and felt anger towards, others who pulled her away from her goal, the goal recognised that it was Melissa herself that had made decisions that kept them apart.

The goal felt no anger, only sadness and frustration.

The debriefing suggests several alternative choreographies that can be played out.

1. *What if the goal moves closer to Melissa as Melissa moves along with Nicholas and Olivia? This would represent Melissa changing her goal as she moves along in life.*

2. *What if Melissa stops Nicholas and points out her goal to him? This would represent Melissa sharing her goal with colleagues so that they can understand she has goals that differ from theirs? This could lead to win-win compromises.*

3. *What if Melissa's goal comes forward, takes Nicholas's arm and presents herself to him? This case is not quite so clear but would probably represent Melissa presenting her goal to Nicholas in an attempt to interest him in sharing her goal.*

4. *What if Melissa runs away from Nicholas and Olivia and towards her goal? This would represent Melissa changing her life to focus on pursuing her goal. As alternative, what if Melissa runs away from Nicholas, Olivia and her goal and in a completely different direction? This would represent Melissa starting afresh in her professional life.*

Depending on Melissa's feelings, some or all of these scenarios could be performed as choreographies followed by debriefings that discuss not only the physical actions, but the feelings, motivations, fears and aspirations of all concerned (including inanimate objects like goals or careers or photocopiers).

Melissa proposes a choreography in which she flees Nicholas and Olivia, goes to her goal and then they move to a different position slightly closer to Nicholas and Olivia. This suggests that Melissa needs to leave her current professional work and pursue her goal, albeit in a new direction. At the same time, she does not want to give up the knowledge and connections she has made in her current work.

In performing the choreography, it becomes apparent that if Melissa were suddenly to flee, it would cause anger and confusion in Nicholas and Olivia, but that Melissa would feel empowered and energised while her goal would feel happier.

With this information, Melissa works out how to make the choreographed situation happen in her real life which means leaving her job and starting something new. From the choreography, she understands that she needs to communicate with her colleagues and leave her job on good terms – to avoid upsetting them. She may not immediately care about their emotions, but Melissa is astute enough to realise she may have professional relationships with them and her ex-employer in the future.

She also realises that she needs to be flexible with her goal. She is a different woman now than she was a few years ago when she established her professional goals, and she can modify her goals as she grows older and wiser, accordingly.

PLAYING WITH THE SITUATION IS THE KEY

The key to creativity is not in having ideas, but in understanding, exploring and playing with a transcendental situation. Often, especially if the
situation does not require complex action, playing with the situation alone
reveals a compelling creative action you could take. In such situations,
particularly if you are working alone or with a small team, you can immediately move onto playing with ideas (see chapter of the same name).

If your situation is more complex or you are involving a larger group
in the idea development phase, then you will need a shared sexy goal.

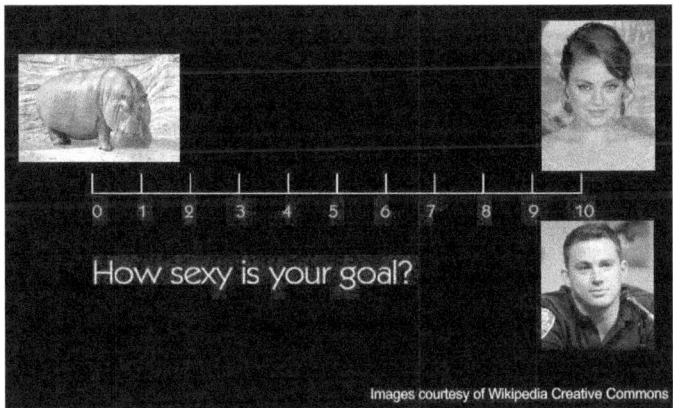

Chart for measuring sexy goals

STEP 2: SEXY GOAL (OPTIONAL)

If you are collaborating in a group or wish to involve others in idea building, I recommend that you formulate a sexy goal which can become the focus for your next step of building a creative vision. A sexy goal focuses thinking on the situation, encourages creativity and ensures everyone is on the same page.

In ACT, we work with a goal whereas CPS and brainstorming use problem statements as the focus for idea generation. There are three reasons we prefer goals in ACT:

1. You merely solve problems – and then you are finished. You can aim to surpass goals.

2. Working towards a goal generates a positive feeling and a sense of moving forward.

3. Problems are for losers and goals are for winners; you are a winner!

A sexy goal is one that is provocative, desirable and interesting. A good sexy goal helps to make people think differently about the situation, which enables their minds to connect unexpected notions with the situation. For example, imagine you are tasked with designing a new camera for your company. Typical problem/challenge statements are: "In what ways might we improve upon our existing cameras?" or "What features might we include on our new camera?" These are fine problem statements, but they are conventional and focused on cameras. The result will surely be conventional camera ideas.

A sexy goal would be: "Describe a device that allows people to capture and share memories!" Do you see how this frees the mind from thinking about cameras and makes it easier to come up with creative, unconventional ideas?

Once you have formulated your first sexy goal, ask yourself if it is sexy (or extreme) enough. I can tell you already that it is not, so get sexier. In my workshops, I use the chart at the beginning of this chapter – using images of sexy celebrities (according to the media) – to enable participants to rate how sexy their goal is. If their goal is not an eight or higher on the scale, I insist they push their goals harder.

SAMPLE SEXY GOALS

Here some examples of typical brainstorm challenges or problem statements and sexy goal alternatives.

Problem Statement/Challenge
How might we improve our healthcare services? (Chain of medical clinics)

Sexy Goal
How can we ensure our patients are by far the healthiest in the country?

Problem Statement/Challenge
How might we increase the appeal of medium-size pick-up trucks to women? (Car and light truck manufacturer)

Sexy Goal
Design the perfect transportation for a woman who occasionally needs to carry a couple cubic metres of cargo.

Problem Statement/Challenge
In what ways might we encourage our citizens to eat more healthily and exercise more? (Government campaign to reduce obesity)

Sexy Goal

It is 2025, and our country made global headlines for having the highest percentage of healthy citizens on the planet. Our men and women all have thin to average well-toned bodies, exercise regularly and have excellent overall health. What have we done to make this happen?

TRICKS FOR SEXINESS

There are several tricks you can use to formulate a sexy goal.

Core Value

Put the goal in the context of the relevant core value. As Theodore Levitt, a marketing professor at Harvard University, famously said, "People do not want to buy a quarter-inch drill. They want a quarter inch-hole." When it comes time to build new drill products, do not ask, "In what ways might we improve our drills?" Instead, set a goal of "Making it easier to make better quarter inch holes."

Superlatives and Extremes

Use superlatives and extremes to make a goal sexy. Instead of asking how you might improve a product, ask how to make it the best product of its kind in the universe. Instead of asking for ideas to simplify a process, ask what you need to do to make the process so easy a drunk mouse could do it blindfolded.

Other People's Perspectives

Because we are the ones who will implement, or at least oversee the implementation, of an idea, we have a tendency to look at goals from our own perspectives. Formulating the goal from the perspective of someone else, such as your customers, can be very sexy. "What would make our customers love shopping with us?"

Of course, you can also put the goal in the perspective of someone, or an organisation, which has nothing to do with you. "If McDonald's was in this situation, what would they do?" If you are Burger King, this is not sexy. But if you are a corporate law firm, it could be very sexy and will certainly generate original ideas.

Threats

Threats demand attention and change the way one thinks. Compare, "How might we improve our product to gain market share over the competition?" to "Describe a new product our competitor could announce tomorrow that would put us out of business by the end of the year?" Which of these is more likely to inspire truly creative thinking?

Unusual Metaphors

Metaphors are a great way to make new and unexpected connections between notions in your mind. Need to launch a new, trendy mobile phone for young people? Set the goal to "Design a mobile phone that feels like holding your sweetheart's hand." Or, "How could we make our customers' shopping experience as delightful as eating chocolate?"

Emotions

Including emotions in a non-emotional situation or to inanimate things can be inspiring in unexpected ways. For example, "How might we make our product adore our customers?" Or, "How might we make our e-commerce website feel more confident about itself?"

Including emotions helps make people think about situations from new perspectives, which brings new notions to an existing situation.

SEXY GOALS LEAD TO SEXY THINKING

Typical challenge statements used in brainstorms and similar events may be well crafted to elicit the right kinds of ideas. But they tend to be boring and uninspiring. As a result, they lead to boring, conventional thinking. Sexy goals, on the other hand, elicit sexy ideas, which more readily form the building blocks of an unconventional, creative vision.

Devising and framing sexy goals is a creative act in its own right and a place where a facilitator can add significant value to an ACT session.

ONE FINAL NOTE

In some cultures the term "sexy goal" may not be appropriate. In such cases, I recommend using the term "extreme goal" which conveys a similar meaning without the sexy bit.

STEP 3: PLAYING WITH IDEAS

Many creative thinking techniques, such as brainstorming, creative problem solving, brainwriting (a technique in which each individual in a group writes ideas on a sheet of paper and then passes the paper to another; each person writes new ideas on each list she receives) and approximately a zillion others operate under the assumption that the only way to devise a creative idea is to encourage a group of people to generate as many ideas as possible, without criticising or questioning any of those apparently precious ideas. According to this model of creativity, people initially spew out lots of boring, conventional ideas. But once they run out of those, they will have no choice but to come up with creative ideas.

It's a lovely concept with one minor flaw; it makes no sense whatsoever. Look at it this way: imagine you are at a dinner party sitting next to a man who tells you boring, very predictable stories from his life. You have several choices. You could, of course, sit and politely listen to him all evening in hopes that once he runs out of boring stories, he will have no choice but to start telling original and interesting stories. But do you really think that will happen?

Alternatively, you could try and find another, more interesting conversation within earshot. But, that would be rude and might not be possible. It could, after all, be a boring dinner party.

The third option would be to provoke the man into being more interesting by asking him unusual questions that force him to rethink one of his stories and turn it into a grand, exciting and original adventure.

ONE CREATIVE VISION

That is essentially the ideation concept of ACT. We do not make long lists of ideas. We do not stick Post-It notes all over a room and each other. We build a single creative vision by provoking ourselves to be creative.

In ACT, we play with ideas, question ideas, criticise ideas, reject ideas that seem boring, trash ideas that are not viable and build upon unconventional ideas in order to make them more and more creative with the aim of developing not a list of ideas, but a single, sophisticated creative vision constructed with smaller ideas.

This gives ACT three huge advantages over most other creative thinking methods that emphasise generating lots of ideas.

1. Building just one creative vision is a lot more efficient than collecting a long list of ideas, most of which will have to be rejected later.

2. If you have only one idea or creative vision, you can get to work on implementing it immediately. If you have a long list of ideas, you still need to reduce the list size, combine ideas and select ideas before you can go further.

3. A creative vision is much more sophisticated and detailed than an idea or even a list of varied ideas.

Before we can go into the process behind building a creative vision, we need to revisit two fundamental rules of ACT.

THE FIRST FUNDAMENTAL RULE OF ACT

Before you begin to play with and build ideas in ACT, you must bear in mind the fundamental rule: boring ideas are prohibited. They are not allowed. Not at all. Absolutely not.

If you are participating in an ACT session and you feel a boring idea forming in your mind, you must stifle it. If necessary, cover your mouth to hold it in. If you are working with a team and someone else suggests a boring idea, you must criticise it immediately, before it contaminates your ACT session, and everyone gets boring!

It can be useful to have a "Boring Ideas Prohibited" sign (like the one above) to remind people of this most fundamental rule.

WHY THIS ANTI-BORING IDEA OBSESSION?

You may wonder why ACT is so vehemently against boring ideas. The answer is simple; you need to program your Mental Bureaucrat (whom we met earlier in this book) to change its usual behaviour. As you will recall, in normal day to day life, the Mental Bureaucrat watches over your thinking and behaviour. He rejects thinking that is too unusual and which might cause you embarrassment, such as sharing a stupid idea. Since it is often very difficult to determine whether an original, unconventional idea is creative or stupid, your Mental Bureaucrat is likely to kill the unconventional idea to be on the safe side. Clearly, a mind that is rejecting unusual ideas does your creative thinking potential no good!

So, you need to make it clear to the Mental Bureaucrat that in the current situation, sharing a boring, conventional idea would be bad for you while sharing a crazy, unconventional, possibly stupid, but possibly brilliant idea is good for you.

In short, prohibiting boring ideas reprograms your Mental Bureaucrat and Reprogramming your Mental Bureaucrat is critical in ACT. It is a key difference between ACT and many other creative thinking techniques, which tend to promote generating lots of ideas, provide no instructions to your Mental Bureaucrat and, as a result, lead to a lot of boring, conventional ideas without necessarily encouraging crazy, unconventional, possibly stupid ideas. After all, in these techniques, the Mental Bureaucrat is given no special instructions and so is likely to operate as normal.

The Second Fundamental Rule of ACT

This points to the other fundamental rule of ACT: you can and should criticise ideas. However, you must follow the rules of criticism.

1. Always criticise boring ideas.

2. Criticise the idea, not the person.

3. Once you have criticised an idea, you must shut up and let the originator of the idea or anyone else defend the idea.

In addition to the three rules of criticism, there are three recommendations.

1. Try to formulate criticism as questions.

2. Try to suggest an alternative idea or an improvement whenever you criticise an idea.

3. If an idea is insufficiently unconventional, ask how to make it madder, crazier, more insane.

If you have been trained in conventional creative thinking methods, this embrace of criticism might come as a surprise. You may even feel it is wrong. However, research and my own experience have shown that not only can you be creative when criticism of ideas is encouraged, you can actually be far more creative.

In the chapter "The Problem with Brainstorming," I go into the research on why criticism is a good thing when you are collaborating for creativity. However, a participant in one of my ACT workshops summed it up nicely: "when we are allowed to criticise ideas, we can really question them and really understand them." And that is very true. If you are in a traditional brainstorm and someone suggests an idea that does not make sense to you, you have no choice but to leave it on the list of ideas (most likely to be rejected later). However, if you can stop and say, "That idea does not make sense to me," then the person suggesting the idea can explain her thoughts. As a result, you may realise the idea is a very good one that was simply expressed poorly. You might even decide to build the idea up further.

On the other hand, if the idea is not suitable for your situation, you can discuss why the idea does not work. As a result, you and the team learn something that will help you in developing your creative vision.

You may be concerned that allowing people to criticise ideas will result in hurt feelings and stifled creativity. In my experience, this is not the case at all. In fact, the worst thing you can do to an idea is to ignore it. That tells the originator that the idea is not worth thinking about. By stopping to discuss an individual's idea, you are actually giving the idea value. You are saying, in effect, "your idea is interesting enough that we need to talk about it." That is much more of a compliment than ignoring an idea and striking it off a list of ideas later.

Lastly, the only way you can truly build upon an idea is by first questioning and criticising it. After all, building upon an idea is, in effect, saying the original idea was not good enough; something you are forbidden to say in most creative thinking methods. In ACT, you can point out weaknesses in an idea and suggest ways to overcome the weakness.

Alternatively, you may recognise that an idea simply will not work and why; information that will help you come up with better, workable ideas right away. For instance, if a great idea would cost far more than your budget permits, you can reject the idea and focus on more cost-effective ideas during idea generation – rather than waste time dreaming up more expensive ideas.

On a final note, I have noticed that when people are encouraged to criticise ideas, the result is a far more lively, animated and involved discussion than when people simply make long lists of ideas, forbidden to question any of them.

Building Ideas Through Play

To visualise how a creative vision is built in ACT, it is useful to imagine two teams of kids, each with a massive set of Lego® building bricks and the goal of building a model for an original, creative and fun school bus. One team makes a long list of school bus ideas. No ideas are criticised. All ideas are welcome. Eventually, they combine similar ideas into bigger ideas and then vote to decide the best idea. Once they have done that, they can build their idea.

Meanwhile, the other team just starts building a vehicle by putting bricks together and seeing what happens. Sometimes the entire team works together. Sometimes an individual works independently on a component of the vehicle. Occasionally, the children try to build something, only to find the idea does not work. So, they remove those bricks and try something else.

As they work, they discuss their ideas, criticise ideas they think will not work and, especially, reject boring ideas. Their aim is to make an original, creative and fun school bus, not a conventional, boring school bus!

The first group follows the traditional creative problem-solving method – that leaves them with a list of ideas. The second group are effectively using the ACT method: they are building a single, elaborate, model or creative vision.

This is how ACT works. It is not a method for generating ideas, but a method for building a creative vision in which you use ideas rather like bricks: ideas are simply building blocks for a creative vision.

MODEL A VISION

In an ACT session, you can use construction toys like Lego® building bricks, wooden building blocks, craft-making materials, clay or any other kit that allows people to make models. Such modelling of a vision has a couple of advantages over using words.

1. It enables the entire team to work together continually. People do not have to stop and listen to ideas. They do not have to wait. They can simply build.

2. People who might be less eloquent or less fluent (such as anyone who does not speak the shared language as her own first language) can more easily participate than if they have to formulate their thoughts into words.

3. A model of a vision is easier to present to others and explain, which is particularly useful when selling a concept to managers, customers or business partners.

Vision modelling is particularly suitable for situations that involve physical objects, such as product innovation or packaging innovation. However, model building can also be used for more abstract concepts such as internal communications, building networks and customer service. In scenarios such as these, participants can be instructed to build representations of communications lines or networks, for example.

BUILDING A VISION WITH WORDS

Of course, you can also use words to build creative visions. Nevertheless, the process is the same: you play with ideas and piece them together to build a vision. Initially, group members throw out ideas that are discussed and criticised as necessary. Once an idea takes hold, the group can build upon it, making additional suggestions that work towards transforming the idea into a creative vision.

Each idea can be discussed, criticised and further developed. Alternatively, it can be rejected. If the creative vision starts to seem non-viable, you can back up and change the details. You can even give up on the creative vision and start again.

Just as children use building bricks to build a creative model through trial and error, you can use verbal ideas to build a creative vision through trial and error.

THE DANCE TROUPE

The managers of the Erps-Kwerps Dance Troupe meet to discuss their next perform-ance, which is to be in three months' time. Evelyn, the producer, starts the discussion. "As you know, the renovation of our auditorium is nearly complete and our next show will be the first to use the new space, so I think we should come up with a special per-formance to mark the occasion. Any suggestions?"

"How about Romeo and Juliet?" asks William, the choreographer.

"That's so boring!" exclaims Jennifer, the stage designer. "Romeo and Juliet has been done to death. Let's do something different."

"That's true," agrees William. "But Shakespeare's themes can be powerful and a real challenge."

"I know, let's do King Lear!" suggests Anna, the music director already thinking about some powerful Bach she could use.

"Yes, King Lear is powerful, and my favourite Shakespeare play," agrees Robert,

the stage designer. "But do you think it is too depressing for one of our dance perform-ances? I reckon we want something a little more uplifting. What do you think?"

"Maybe we can do depressing with an uplifting ending," says Anna thoughtfully.

"Hey, let's combine lovers and depressing to make a black comedy," says William.

"What do you have in mind?" asks Evelyn.

"Two lovers at the end of the world. They initially do not like each other, but slowly come together," says William.

"End of the world?" exclaims Evelyn. "That's hardly uplifting."

"Well, the lovers come together at the end," says William.

"I don't know," begins Evelyn, thinking.

"Actually, a post-apocalyptic stage could be great fun to design," says Robert.

"Yeah, and I could have a lot of fun designing some end of the world dances," agrees William.

"Hey, maybe the lovers could become the Adam and Eve of a new human race," says Anna.

"Yeah, this is beginning to work!" says Evelyn. "So, are we going to include the ending of the world in the dancing?"

"No, I think the show should start in the immediate aftermath. I can see the stage now. It is littered with broken rubble; steel girders jut up here and there. Smoke is rising," says Robert.

This conversation continues for a while until the dance troupe has a solid outline for their next performance. Now each of them gets to work on her or his part. Willi-am starts on the choreography. Anna works on the music and so on.

As you can see, the dance troupe has a conversation in which they play with ideas, trying them out in their minds and through discussion. They question ideas, reject ideas and, once they find an idea they like, they build upon it – in much the same way children might collaborate on building something.

Within a couple of hours, they have an outline of a dance perform-ance, which means they can all get to work immediately.

You can use this approach effectively for almost any situation. It is a simple process of suggesting ideas, playing with those ideas, rejecting them or building upon them – all the while focusing on rejecting conven-tional, boring ideas.

And if unconventional ideas do not flow, it may help to identify the conventional ideas first and work from there as we will see in the next chapter.

PROHIBITED IDEAS

A great way to ensure that you do not waste time with boring, conventional ideas is to start the idea play by making a list of conventional actions you might take in the situation and using them as a basis for developing unconventional ideas. It is a simple trick that can be surprisingly effective.

Start by making a short list of conventional, obvious ideas for your given situation. The easiest way to do this is probably a mini-brainstorm. Formulate your situation as a traditional brainstorm challenge and generate ideas for 10 minutes or so. Most of the ideas you come up with are likely to be conventional ones. That's good, but if you should come up with a truly creative idea, set it aside for later. Meanwhile, combine related conventional ideas, reformulate them into broader ideas as necessary and list them on a sheet of poster paper, a white board or a notebook page depending on your preference and whether you are collaborating or working alone.

Now, draw a big, red circle around this list of ideas. These are prohibited ideas. You are not allowed to voice or write down ideas that fall in the prohibited ideas category.

As ideas come to mind, you can test them against the prohibited ideas list. If an idea is similar to one of the prohibited ones, you need to reject it and try again.

If you are stuck for ideas or your ideas are not unconventional enough, go through the prohibited ideas and for each one, ask:

1. What is the opposite of this prohibited idea? Note, there may be more than one opposite.

2. Take this prohibited idea to such an extreme that your idea is no longer a prohibited idea.

3. Turn the prohibited idea around to change its meaning. This is not always possible, but when it is, it can be very interesting.

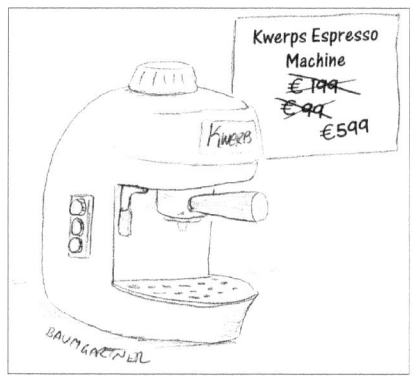

ESPRESSO MACHINES

Kwerps, a leading manufacturer of coffee makers is facing a challenge. Their best selling product, an espresso machine that has been on the market for some years, is looking a bit out of date and is losing market share to capsule coffee makers (such as Nespresso). Emily, the product manager, puts together a small team to come up with creative ideas for rebuilding market share and revenues of the espresso machine.

The team quickly brainstorms a list of conventional ideas that they combine and reformulate into a short list:

1. *Reduce prices in order to sell more machines.*

2. *Update the design, so our machines look newer.*

3. *Add capsule functionality.*

4. *Add new features.*

There is nothing wrong with these ideas, except that they are conventional, and Emily absolutely does not want conventional ideas. So, Emily draws a red circle around the ideas. They are prohibited ideas.

Then they go through the ideas starting with the first one.

Prohibited, boring idea: *reduce prices to sell more machines.*

Opposite: *increase prices. How might the team do this? They could re-position the espresso machine as a high-quality classic espresso maker for traditionalists. Their next steps would then be to re-engineer the machine with better quality components and to emphasise its slightly out of date, classic appearance.*

Extreme 1: *give the coffee machines away free. How might the team do this? They could partner with a coffee distributor and offer a subscription service in which customers pay for quality coffee to be sent to their house, and they get a free coffee maker in exchange. This might be modelled after the way many mobile telephone contracts work.*

Extreme 2: *make the coffee machines incredibly expensive; price them at the same level as a luxury car. How might the team do this? They could use super high quality parts, add some gold or diamonds to it. Include regular servicing by a technician for the first three years in the price. Guarantee if for 50 years. Note that this action would result in reduced sales and market share, but if it worked, Kwerps could expect significantly higher margins per sale, which would result in more revenue and a better reputation in the market.*

Turn prohibited idea around in order to change its meaning: *"reduce machines in order to sell more at a price." How might the team do this? Perhaps they could make a pocket-sized espresso maker that attaches to the tap so there is no need for a water reservoir. It would be ideal for travel, keeping in the office, camping and small kitchens.*

As you can see, using the prohibited, conventional ideas as a springboard for developing unconventional ideas is an easy way to get creative. Moreover, as you develop ideas in reaction to the prohibited ideas list, you will soon find other ideas developing in your mind. As this happens, check those ideas against the list. If your ideas are too similar to the prohibited ones, you must either reject the idea or modify it so that it differs significantly from the prohibited ideas list.

Using the prohibited ideas list, you will almost certainly find powerful, unconventional ideas that can be built into visions.

TESTING AND PRESENTING A CREATIVE VISION

Once you have built your creative vision, you will need to present it to others. You can, of course, make a point-by-point description and explain your vision. You could even present it in a PowerPoint presentation rich in bullet points. But, let's be honest, that would be rather boring and hardly in keeping with the concept of ACT!

There are better ways to present your vision, which are not only more creative, but which allow you to test your vision. Telling a story, building a model (or presenting a model if you used that approach to ACT) and role-plays are great ways to present and test creative visions.

TELL A STORY

Put your creative vision into a story. We human beings tend to enjoy stories, so presenting your vision as a story can be compelling in ways that are particularly useful if you need people, such as managers or customers, to buy into your idea. As you develop the story, you also test it. If the story does not make sense, for example because it requires characters in the story to act in ways that real people are unlikely to act, it suggests you need to address aspects of your vision.

If there is a need to sell the vision to customers, investors or others, consider illustrating your story. Graphic recorders are specialists who record meetings and other events graphically. One could be hired to listen to your story and draw graphic illustrations that could then be used in documenting and presenting the vision.

The Kwerps software company specialises in customer relationship management software and have decided to build a module for managing social media marketing. Following an ACT session, the development team come up with an intelligent agent that guides users through the use of social media and an integration tool that connects to the main social media, facilitating submission of posts and providing clever reporting tools.

To market the software to customers, the team devises a story about a medium-sized, traditional family run firm that finds its market share is shrinking. The firm invests in this new module and, thanks to an effective social media marketing campaign, not only regains market share, but increases it substantially. The story describes the firm, the challenges it faces, the adoption of the software, initial challenges, and eventual success. Within the story is not only a description of the new software module, but a description of how a client might use it – giving the design team insights they might not gain through listing ideas.

BUILD A MODEL

A great way to build a creative vision, especially if you are working on a material concept such as a new product or new packaging, is to build a model of your vision.

Depending on the nature of the vision, the audience to whom the idea will be presented and timing, then you may wish to build a higher quality prototype based on the model built during the idea play stage of the ACT session. For instance, in your ACT session, your team uses Styrofoam, paper, pieces of wood and other craft material to build a vision for an electronic gadget. You might decide to build a working prototype to present your vision to management.

In some cases, you may develop ideas verbally, but wish to present the vision in the form of a model.

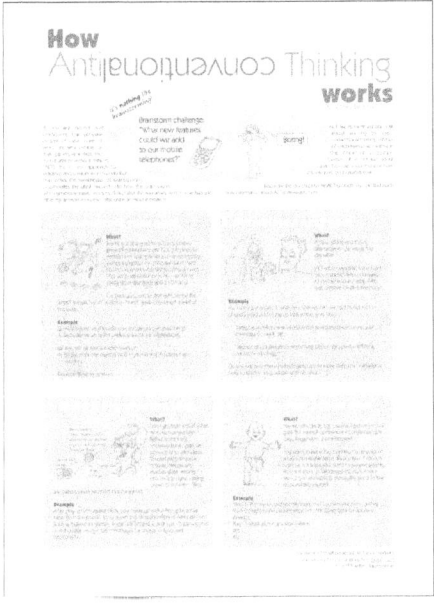

INFOGRAPHICS

The use of infographics (illustrated charts or diagrams) is an increasingly popular way of presenting information that can also be used to present a creative vision. Infographics are particularly useful for presenting process or presenting stories.

Infographics can be used in reports, slide presentations and posters –

all of which are handy for presenting a vision, especially if the team cannot be present to explain their thoughts.

An infographic can complement other forms of idea presentation. For instance, you might tell a story about a vision or show a prototype. You can then leave the infographic as souvenir or reminder of your vision. This is useful if you are presenting your vision to a middle manager rather than the final decision maker.

ROLE-PLAY

Role-plays are especially good for testing creative visions that involve people. Once the vision is well developed, you and your team act it out among yourselves. In so doing, you can expect to identify potential weaknesses in the vision and address them.

The Kwerps Industrial Cleaning supplies company is exploring new business models. In the past, the company focused on sales of cleaning machinery, tools and chemicals. Allison and her team, which includes people from a handful of different divisions, do an ACT session to explore new business model possibilities.

The team's vision is to start marketing service based contracts that include leasing of machinery, servicing, supply of chemicals and training. Each contract includes numerous options to customers, who can pick and choose the services that they need.

To test their concept, the team does a role-play in which the sales people, who are familiar with the kinds of objections potential customers often make, play customers and product developers play sales people presenting the concept to customers.

During the role-play, they discover that explaining a complex choice of services is confusing not only to customers, but to the sales people! So the team rethinks the business model and settles on a simpler choice of contracts, each with a fun name. Trying the role-play again, they find that their new idea works better not only in terms of explaining the new business model to customers, but also explaining to their own colleagues!

ONE VISION

To sum up, the idea generation in ACT is different to idea generation in most other creative thinking methodologies, especially collaborative methods. Other approaches focus on generating and listing a lot of ideas in hopes of finding a usable creative idea afterwards. These methods mostly follow the divergence-convergence model in which you supposedly think divergently by generating a lot of ideas in a free-flowing environment. Later, you converge by choosing one or more ideas from the list.

However, the diverge-converge methods do not address the way the mind builds ideas, and so they result in lots of conventional ideas and few, if any, truly creative ideas.

ACT is a model of playing with ideas in order to build a creative vision. In ACT, you purposefully reject conventional ideas in order to programme your mind to think anticonventionally. In truth, ACT also results in a lot of ideas. However, you evaluate them in real time as they come to mind, and reject the conventional, boring and irrelevant ideas immediately. There is no need to document boring ideas – that only encourages you and others in an ACT session to start thinking conventionally, which is something you do not want.

In keeping with this focus, ACT not only allows criticism of ideas, but encourages it. Again, this focuses the mind on thinking unconventionally, while still focusing on the situation for which you are building a vision.

The result is a single creative vision which you can get to work on immediately. In the next section, we look at how you get to work on a vision through planning.

STEP 4: IMPLEMENTATION PLANNING

One of the problems with a big, bold, creative vision is that while it seems great when you are devising it, it can seem awfully intimidating when it comes time to implement it. This is doubly true if you are doing an ACT session in a business context. What seems like jolly good fun in a relaxed, off-site creativity event, can suddenly seem like a burden once you've returned to your desk where you find urgent, unanswered emails, meeting requests and a to-do list that doubled in size while you were away. Often, these tasks have deadlines while your creative vision does not.

Not surprisingly, without determination or preliminary implementation planning, most creative visions never move on from vision to reality. The situation is made worse when the implementation team includes more than one person; typically each awaits the others to take action and, as a result, action does not happen.

If a creative vision is conceptually too big and, therefore, intimidating when it comes time to implement it, you clearly need to make it smaller. You can do that by breaking the implementation of the vision into a series of smaller, manageable steps that you can tackle one at a time.

However, before you dive into implementation planning, there are a few things to keep in mind. Let's look at them.

GOAL!

Once you have decided to realise your creative vision, it's implementation can and should be considered a goal. Conceptually, this changes the way you think about your vision, from a great idea to a goal that you can achieve.

Moreover, there is a lot of information available on achieving goals. You can use this material to guide you on your path to implementation. Indeed, the ACT process steals best practice of personal development and attaining goals. However, the ACT does two things differently. Firstly, the ACT process also allows for greater flexibility, because creative visions can be more complex and uncertain than personal goals. Secondly, the ACT process is usually performed by teams rather than individuals, and there are a couple of things you need to do differently when a team, rather than an individual, is responsible for the goal.

BE FLEXIBLE

When it comes to implementation plans, you need to be flexible. As you draw up yours, you may feel the need to modify details of your creative vision to facilitate its implementation and, perhaps to improve the vision. As long as the modifications do not make the vision boring or reduce the vision's ability to meet your needs, this is fine.

When you go on to implement your vision, you are even more likely to have reason to make changes in the vision; especially if your vision is truly creative and original which, by definition, implies the implementation of the vision is untested and involves doing things differently than you have done in the past. Hence, it is hardly surprising that, as you implement your vision, some steps will not be as easy to accomplish as expected; you may discover new ways of accomplishing some steps; and you may even see reason to alter aspects of your vision.

As long as the changes have no adverse effect on the vision and do not make it boring, there is nothing to worry about. Go ahead and make the changes.

Be flexible as you draw up your implementation plan and maintain that flexibility as you implement it.

MANAGE RISK WITH MILESTONES

If the goal is elaborate, requires a significant investment or will have bad consequences if it fails, you should include milestones in your implementation plan. A milestone is some kind of reference point against which you can measure progress.

As you implement your vision and come to each milestone, stop, review progress and determine whether or not you have met the terms of the milestone. If not, you must review the project, determine what went wrong and determine whether you can fix the situation or whether you should kill the implementation and work on a new, creative project.

Do not be too quick to kill a project. Creative projects are unpredictable and may take longer to get off the ground than other projects. But do not hang on to a project that is clearly failing. To do so only prevents you from working on another project that may have a greater chance of succeeding.

Be careful about emotional attachment to a creative project. This easily happens and can skew your perception of the project's viability.

Whether to kill or continue a project that falls short of expectations at a milestone can be a difficult decision. Make it easier on yourself and the implementing team by designing good milestones.

And, if you are not sure whether to kill or continue a project, ask yourself: could the resources of myself and my team be better used on another, possibly more promising project?

But Do Not Kill the Unconventionality

The problem with changes in a creative vision, changes in planning and establishing milestones is that you can inadvertently strip a creative vision of its creativity by making details more conventional. The result is that what starts out as a creative vision can all too easily become a very conventional reality.

The Flying Car that Did Not Fly

Barney, the head of Research and Development bursts into the CEO's office. "I've done it, I've done it!" he shouts, waving a strange looking model in front of Sarah, the CEO.

"What is it?" asks Sarah.

"Why, it's a flying car that operates via a highly efficient fuel cell. The fuel cell runs on water and produces virtually no pollution!"

"A flying car ... That is interesting! But I wonder if our customers would like it. After all, they've been buying wheeled cars from us for nearly a century. Perhaps you could put some wheels on it in order to make it more acceptable to them."

Barney goes back to the drawing board and adds some small wheels to his flying car.

Meanwhile, his creative vision is sent from one review committee to another, and additional changes are made to his design.

"It might be difficult for customers to refill water in the middle of the desert. Perhaps we should also install a petrol [gasoline] engine just in case," says one committee member.

"The wheels look nice and would comfort our buyers, but we think you should make them bigger and allow the flying car to drive as well as fly as there could be times when our customers would not like to fly," says another committee member.

"We feel that having a petrol engine and a fuel cell engine is redundant. Our customers are more used to petrol engines, and we have a very fuel efficient 2.0 litre engine available. So let's drop the fuel cell all together," says another committee member.

"Our legal department is concerned that flying cars could raise liability issues in the event of a crash. Since the car has wheels anyway, they recommend we postpone the flying functionality for a few years until the legal environment is clearer. Let's look at the flying bit again in 2025," says yet another committee member.

"Why don't we try to make the flying car look more like a Mercedes Benz?" asks one more committee member.

And within a few weeks, Barney's truly creative vision of a flying car is replaced by an ordinary petrol-engined car that looks vaguely like a Mercedes Benz.

THE IMPLEMENTATION PLAN

Sometimes a creative vision is so simple to implement that the implementation plan looks like this:

> **Implementation Plan**
> 1. Do it.

However, this is seldom the case. Assuming your vision is more complex, you need to deconstruct it into much smaller steps, or sub-goals, each of which is as simple (or nearly as simple) as the one above, and which together plot a path from where you are now to the achievement of your goal of realising your vision.

GETTING STARTED

The best way to do this is to commandeer a big table. Take a couple of sheets of paper. On one, write, "you are here" in a circle – like you see on those maps on signboards on city streets and nature trails. On another sheet of paper, write down your goal in a few words. Put one sheet at either end of the table.

Now, get a stack of small sheets of paper: index cards, notepad sheets or – if you want to be environmentally friendly – used printer paper cut into quarters. Look at "you are here" and look at your goal and think about what actions you need to take in order to get from "you are here" to your goal. Write down each envisioned action on one of the small papers and put it in the middle of the table in rough order, that is with the first tasks nearer to "you are here" and the latter ones closer to the goal. Do not worry about precision at this time. Focus on writing down the steps and putting them on the table.

STRUCTURE

Once you have exhausted your mind of necessary steps, reorganise them as necessary. You should now have a path of pieces of paper from "you are here" to your goal. Look at your path and each action. Are there redundant actions? If so, remove them. Are there gaps in the path? If so, look at the actions on either side of the gap, think about what action needs to be taken in order to bridge the gap. Write the action down and add it to the path.

Envision performing each step. How do you feel about it? Is it an easy action to implement? If so, that's great! If it is complicated or overwhelming, you probably need to deconstruct that action into smaller steps.

If a step feels intimidating, ask yourself why. Perhaps it obliges you to make a presentation to a large group of people – an action that frightens you. Perhaps it obliges you to ask a favour of someone you do not like. Perhaps it asks you to do something ethically questionable. If so, rethink the action. Can you REALLY do it? If not, find an alternative method of performing this step. Because if you leave it in the sequence of steps and you are unable to perform the action, you will endanger the implementation of your vision. Better to deal with difficult steps in advance, when you are feeling optimistic (you are feeling optimistic, aren't you?) rather than leave them for later.

On the other hand, if a step merely puts you outside of your comfort zone, then keep it in the sequence, but think about whether additional action is necessary. For instance, if you have to give a public presentation, but that makes you uncomfortable, then you might add an additional step, such as signing up for a public speaking training course or joining toastmasters (a club for practising public speaking).

IDENTIFY OBSTACLES

Identify potential obstacles to each step as well as the goal itself. Do you need to extract budget from a manager who is notorious for not buying into risky projects? Will the legal department need to review your vision before you can implement it? Will it require resources that you cannot provide?

If you can identify obstacles and find ways to work around them, you substantially increase the likelihood your creative vision will become an innovative reality.

FIND SOMETHING FUN IN EACH ACTION

Once you have finalised the steps, go through them again, one by one. For each step, find something fun or positive about performing the action. Sometimes this will be easy. Sometimes it will not. But, if you can find something to look forward to in each step, it will increase the likelihood that you complete and that, in turn, increases the likelihood that your creative vision is realised.

COLLABORATIVE IMPLEMENTATION PLANNING

If you are collaborating on implementing a creative vision, you need to assign responsibilities for each step in the sequence. If you do not, everyone in the group will expect someone else to take action, and nothing will happen!

Decide who is in charge of the overall goal. Very likely it will be you. So, I am going to assume it is you. Put your name on the sheet of paper with the goal written on it and acknowledge to the group that you will oversee and coordinate the implementation of the goal.

Then go to the first step and decide who is responsible for the step. Ask her if she has any concerns about her ability to perform the step. If so, address those concerns as described above. If not, or once the concerns are satisfactorily addressed, ask her "Will you take responsibility for [step 1]?" Ensure she replies in the positive. Then ask her to write her name on the step.

It may seem a bit silly asking someone if she will perform a step and asking her to sign the step. But this ensures each member of the group acknowledges his or her responsibility towards the project and the group which, in turn, increases the likelihood that she performs her part in the project's implementation.

This is important. If one person fails to perform her step, it undermines the implementation of the goal and could kill the project! This happens far more often than it should!

Review Development

In addition to measuring progress against milestones, review overall progress on a regular basis and be prepared to modify steps as necessary. As noted, your goal is untested. As a result, some steps are almost certain not to go exactly as expected. A step may not be achievable. Something may go wrong. A particular step may prove impossible.

Mind you, the unexpected is not always negative. You may find that a particular step works out better than expected. Perhaps it costs far less than expected to implement or brings even better results than anticipated.

In addition, you make discoveries as you progress towards implementing the goal. You may have ideas about how to make the goal better, how to get there faster or how to get even better results. Others may want to help you in implementing your goal. Do not refuse these opportunities simply because you have a plan. Change the plan accordingly. Creativity requires flexibility.

When things do not work out as expected, whether in a positive or a negative way, you will probably need to rethink and very likely modify subsequent steps. Do not be afraid to do this. In extreme cases, you may even need to go back to the table and the pieces of paper in order to re-think the implementation plan. There's nothing wrong with that. Do it, but remember to follow the steps above to ensure new steps are doable and that someone has taken responsibility for each.

VISUALISING YOUR GOAL

If you have read up on personal development, you will recognise aspects of the ACT approach to implementing a vision. That's not surprising. Personal development is about defining and achieving goals – and implementing a vision is pretty much the same thing, but with a lot more creativity added.

However, many self-help gurus suggest that you always keep the goal in mind. They insist that you visualise your goal regularly, think about how wonderful you will feel once you have achieved it and think about the benefits. They claim that this will motivate you towards achieving your goal.

They are wrong.

LAW OF DISTRACTION

Some gurus even cite *the Law of Attraction*, which roughly says that if you think about achieving your goal hard enough, you will attract success, and the universe will somehow make your goal come true. This, of course, is ridiculous. The Universe does not really care about your goals or what you do. And if it did care, it would surely expect you to take responsibility for your own goals.

Moreover, research has shown[4] that if you fantasise about achieving your goal, your mind will start to anticipate the pleasure and satisfaction of success, so much so that it will lose interest in the implementation. In experiments, people who fantasise about achieving their goals are less energised than those who do not, and they are less likely to achieve their goals than those who do not fantasise.

Having only positive thoughts about a fantasised future makes you less likely to see the potential pitfalls and obstacles you will face on the road to achieving your goal, which leaves you less prepared to deal with those pitfalls and obstacles.

GREAT EXPECTATIONS

On the other hand, *expectation* that you will achieve your goal increases the likelihood that you will succeed. Why is this? It is because expectation comes from experience. If you have had similar experiences with positive outcomes, you know what is required and can be more confident about achieving your goal. Thanks to experience, you are also more likely to be aware of – and better prepared for – the pitfalls, obstacles and challenges you will face along the way.

---

4   Gabriele Oettingen, Doris Mayer (2002) "The Motivating Function of Thinking About the Future: Expectations Versus Fantasies" Journal of Personality and Social Psychology, Vol 83(5), 1198-1212

TWO EXAMPLES

ANNA THE VIROLOGIST

Anna is a highly respected and qualified virologist specialising in Hepatitis B and C diagnostics. She has published a number of articles on the topic and shares ownership of a few patents. There are not many people in the world with her expertise, and most of them know each other.

She learns that a major pharmaceutical company is setting up a unit to develop a new Hepatitis B diagnostic tool and wishes to hire a principal scientist to oversee the unit. Anna knows she has the relevant qualifications and sees this as a great opportunity as well as a great challenge. She spends a full day researching her potential employer, updates her CV and writes a cover letter which addresses several points she knows are important to her potential employer.

She asks a couple of friends to critique her application. Once she is satisfied with everything, she emails the application and CV to the manager in charge of the project and calls the next day to ensure he has received the application. A week later, he calls her back, invites her for an interview. After several meetings, she is offered the job and an attractive compensation package. She accepts.

MARTIN THE DESIGNER

Martin is a freelance designer who has previously been employed by design firms. His design work is very good, and his clients are generally happy with his work. He learns that one of the big London design firms is looking for a senior creative director. It is his dream job: good pay, a lot of responsibility and many challenges. He would oversee a team, travel regularly and work with top clients. Of course, Martin does not have management experience, but he's a good designer who gets on well with others. He's sure he'd be a good manager. Martin is soon imagining himself in the job, travelling around the world, having a nice car, hobnobbing with top management at parties, meeting pretty young women who admire him.

He quickly writes a cover letter and emails it, together with his CV, to the design firm. He's sure he'll get the job because it feels right.

In fact, he never hears from them. Pity, it was a cool fantasy.

Do you see the difference? Owing to her background and the nature of the job offer, Anna can reasonably expect to be offered the job. Nevertheless, she realises that she needs to demonstrate her value to her employer. So, she devotes a serious effort to updating her CV and writing a compelling application.

Martin, on the other hand, is busier fantasising about getting the job. Indeed, it starts to seem real to him. As a result, he loses his motivation. He hardly even bothers to fill out an application letter. But that doesn't matter; he probably would not have got the job anyway as he is not sufficiently qualified.

DANGEROUS FANTASIES

Unfortunately, big creative visions, by their nature, are more likely to be outside of your experience. Worse, if you are a creative thinker, you are probably particularly good at having fantasies! So, you need to avoid fantasising or even thinking much about the final goal.

Instead, you need to focus your creative thinking on each step as you tackle it. See the goal as the final destination on the road map and the steps as your route to the destination.

Nothing New Under the Sun

NOTHING NEW UNDER THE SUN

Although ACT is a new structured approach to creativity, it is not really new. I pretty much looked at the way artists, composers, writers, scientists and others think and collaborate. I have the advantage of being a writer and having been an artist as well as having friends in the arts and sciences.

Moreover, I am fortunate in that the recent interest in creativity and innovation in business has led to an explosion of research into all aspects of creativity, from the dynamics of brainstorming to which bits of the brain are most active when improvisational jazz musicians improvise. I've read through loads of research and have been able to apply the findings in laying out an easily followable ACT process. Perhaps not surprisingly, the approach creative people have been using for centuries, if not longer, fits nicely with the science in ways that brainstorming and other idea generation methods do not.

So, to be honest, I pretty much stole the approach artists and others tend to use when being creative, applied some science and created ACT.

ACT is a work in progress. I do workshops around the world, teaching teams how to use ACT in their work. I also facilitate ACT sessions and speak about ACT at conferences and within organisations. Fortunately, I have been able to work with people in Europe, the United States, Asia and the Middle East, which has given me experience using the process with a wide range of cultures and in all kinds of environments in-cluding cutting edge business, traditional business, government and non-profit. I have been delighted to see that irrespective of where people are from, their cultural beliefs or even their religions, they are able to embrace and use ACT.

I am continually learning about ACT and how people use it. This book is the result of three years using, teaching and talking about ACT, and it is pretty solid. Nevertheless, I will surely continue to tweak the process over time.

I will also document the tweaks, which you will always be able to find at www.jpb.com/act.

I would also love to know about your experiences with ACT. Please share them with me at act@jpb.com.

ACKNOWLEDGEMENTS

Firstly, I would like to thank the many brainstorm enthusiasts who regularly criticised ACT, told me repeatedly that I did not understand brainstorming and insisted that research critical of brainstorming was wrong because, well, it was just wrong! Their antagonism gave me the confidence that I was on to something and pushed me to continue to develop ACT. There's nothing like a little antagonism to motivate a guy like me!

More specifically, I would like to thank my friend Fernando Cardoso De Sousa who gave me the opportunity to present ACT at the European Conference on Creativity and Innovation in Faro in 2011 and who brought me in to use ACT for a development project in the Algarve Region of Portugal. This was the first real-world trial of ACT. And it was a successful session in spite of many participants being less than enthusiastic about creativity processes.

I would also like to thank Daksha Bhat, Mukesh Gupta, Gijs van Beeck Calkoen, KK Yew, Lief Almeling, Andrea Eva Nagy, Claude Diderich, Paul Forsythe and Pete Cole who reviewed the draft copy and provided loads of useful advice for improving this book.

Thanks also to my editor, Brian Cross, who cleaned up my typos, spelling errors and other mistakes with remarkable efficiency.

Last, but not least, I'd like to thank my family for their support and just being a really great family!

ABOUT THE AUTHOR

Jeffrey Baumgartner has done a great many things in many places, including being born in the US, studying art in London, teaching English in Lisbon and writing magazine columns in Bangkok; he's also launched an early Internet company, advised the European Commission on e-commerce, and developed an innovation process management software in spite of never formally learning how to code. He is the author of *The Way of the Innovation* Master and *The Insane Journey*, a science fiction humour novel. These days, he writes, facilitates creativity workshops and speaks about innovation globally. He lives and works in Erps-Kwerps, Belgium, a village whose name even the Belgians find funny.